The Versatile Organization:

New Ways of

Thinking About

Your Business

The Versatile Organization:

New Ways of

Thinking About

Your Business

Ruth Tearle

Amsterdam • Johannesburg • Oxford
San Diego • Sydney • Toronto

**Library of Congress
Cataloging-in-Publication Data**

Tearle, Ruth.
 The versatile organization: new ways of thinking
about your business / Ruth Tearle.
    p. cm.
 Includes index.
 ISBN 0-88390-435-7
 1. Organizational effectiveness. 2. Organizational change. I. Title.
HD58.9.T43 1994
658.4'063—dc20   94-1660
              CIP

Printed in the United States of America

Published by Pfeiffer & Company
8517 Production Avenue
San Diego, California 92121-2280
United States of America
1-619-578-5900; FAX 1-619-578-2042

To Sandy who thought it would be a good idea
to write this book. And Sam, Honey, and Lesley
who encouraged me to finish it.

Table of Contents

CHAPTER NINE: Managing the Transition

Introduction

The tools of the mind become burdens when the conditions which give rise to them no longer exist.

—Henri Bergson

Not Another Panacea

Strategic planning, change management, and leadership in a turbulent environment are topics that generate attention in conferences, seminars, and books. Although these are popular topics of conversation, they represent concepts that are extremely difficult to put into practice. This is because the type of organization in which these concepts thrive differs radically from the reality of most organizations.

The Theory

One of the biggest growth industries today is that of consulting to business leaders on managing their organizations more successfully in a changing world. The consulting industry has spawned books, videotapes, training courses, and conferences on managing organizations.

The message from the business consultants during the 1980s was that excellent companies were the ones that:

- Developed clear visions and strategies;

- Fostered cultures of quality and excellence;

- Provided superior customer service;

- Had leaders who managed by "walking around";

- Segmented their markets and provided superior products and services to chosen market segments; and

- Handled labor relations effectively.

Today, successful organizations are described as ones that:

- Understand their customers and anticipate their changing needs;

- Are obsessed with customer responsiveness;

- Focus on and dominate specific markets;

- Provide superior products and services faster and more cheaply than their competitors;

- Build quality into their corporate culture;

- Build a culture of innovation;

- Monitor their environments and create their own futures;

- Become learning environments;

- Have inspired leaders who lead with visions and values;

- Have flexible structures;

- Have a capability to act quickly to exploit environmental changes; and

- Establish strategic alliances.

These ideas make a lot of sense at conferences, and, usually, the attendees leave feeling excited and motivated. But what happens when these changes are introduced into organizations? How many of these programs work?

The Practice

Many programs have been developed to help emulate successful organizations. Consider the following programs and call to mind the ones that your organization has tried to implement:

- Management by objectives,

- Quality circles,

- Total-quality programs,

- Japanese management,

- Employee-empowerment programs,

- Participative management,

- Visions,

- Missions,

- Cultural-change management,

- Customer-focus programs,

- Strategic planning,

- Cross-cultural programs,

- Activity-based budgeting, and

- Performance-management programs.

How many of these programs have really worked? How many of them have followed a life cycle that looks something like the following?

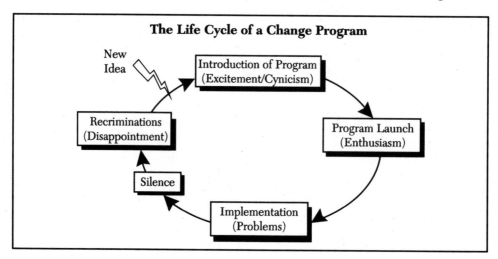

The Life Cycle of a Change Program

Introduction of the Program

During the introduction phase, the program is presented as one that will make the organization more effective and successful in the future. The promoters of the program are excited; those opposing the program are cynical. The potential benefits of the program are discussed.

Program Launch

The program is launched. The program's processes and its benefits are described to the staff. A period of enthusiasm and hard work follows.

Implementation Problems

Problems associated with implementing the program begin to emerge. People find that they have insufficient time to spend on the program. Other priorities, such as doing one's job, become more important. There is resistance to the additional work required to make the program work. People become frustrated and stressed. The ratio between the amount of effort invested in the program and the benefits reaped from it is perceived as being uneven. Some people become cynical. Others suggest that they will commit themselves to the program only when they have seen evidence of other people's commitment. People hear about other new ideas or techniques and want to investigate them even before discussing implementation.

Silence

The person who championed the program is assigned to more important priorities and the program is set aside.

Disappointment/Recriminations

Finally someone reminds the decision makers how much was spent on the program and asks them what benefits were attained. The decision makers and the staff feel disappointed and cheated. The consultant who sold the program to the organization is upset. All agree that the organization meticulously followed the steps involved in implementing the program. Somehow the "spirit" required for successful implementation was lacking. Top management loses patience with the consultant and accepts its losses.

The organization then tries the next "management fad." But are these programs merely fads? Why do change programs work in some organizations and why are they so difficult to implement in others? And what is the "spirit" of implementing a change program?

The Spirit

When I consult with leaders, they often are frustrated by the lack of progress in implementing change programs. Many of them have read books about how well-known organizations have successfully changed. The leaders will then apply the suggested techniques and methodologies meticulously, step-by-step, in their own organizations. They invest a great deal of personal time and energy to make the program work. When such programs fail, the leaders attribute the lack of progress to their middle management, to their employees, or to the program itself.

But something else is missing, something crucial that no one tells the leaders about, namely, the spirit in which the programs are implemented. In this context, I am referring to the invisible rules and assumptions on how organizations operate. Observance of these rules is taken for granted when the program is designed. If they are disregarded during the implementation, the program fails. The problem is that these assumptions are often not discussed. They certainly do not appear in training programs or in business-school curriculum.

The root cause of the problem is that many of the designs underlying today's change programs are based on the assumption that the programs are to be implemented in a specific type of organization—one that I shall call the "versatile organization." The versatile organization differs from traditional organizations in that it perceives itself as operating in an environment that resembles a kaleidoscope—an environment that continually changes its boundaries, relationships, and structures. Versatile organizations thrive in such an environment. They are structured to exploit change and have underlying values and beliefs that are attuned to a turbulent environment.

Every organizational model that has been studied in business school or in the working environment revolves around a different concept of what an organization really is. The traditional hierarchical organization is designed for efficiency and productivity and thrives in a predictable, slowly changing environment.

When an organization superimposes a change program based on a versatile organization onto a traditionally structured organization, confusion, stress, and frustration often result. Transitional organizations are caught between two models and two ages. It is only after leaders unlearn the assumptions regarding traditional hierarchical organizations and embrace the values and beliefs of a versatile organization that they will find change programs easier to implement.

Conclusion

This book will help traditional organizations to understand the transition that their organizations need to experience to be successful. Through an understanding of the underlying assumptions of a versatile organization, as opposed to traditional hierarchical organizations, leaders will be able to understand the causes of stress and confusion in their organizations. They can then consider what needs to be done to manage the transition.

Chapter 1 describes the environment in which organizations are operating at present. Chapter 2 provides a model of a versatile organization operating successfully within a turbulent environment. The features of a versatile organization are described in Chapters 3 to 6. Chapter 7 illustrates the features of traditional organizations. Chapter 8 discusses how confusion results when change programs associated with versatile organizations are superimposed onto traditional organizations. Chapter 9 offers guidance on how leaders can survive the transition from a traditional organization to a versatile organization.

1

The Turbulent Environment

History in the late 20th century seems to belong more to chaos theory and particle physics and fractuals; it moves by bizarre accelerations and illogics, by deconstructions and bursts of light. It features dangerous simultaneities at work: instantaneous planetary communications co-exist with atavistic greeds and hungers.

—Lance Morrow

Introduction

In discussions on the business environment, words such as turbulence, change, chaos, and innovation frequently are used. The events and challenges facing leaders and managers alike have never been experienced before. In facing these challenges, leaders cannot rely on their past experience, education, or training. They cannot rely on ideas and methodologies that assisted them even a few years ago. For the world today differs from that of yesterday. (Also see the Introduction, which further amplifies this point.)

Approaching the 21st Century— A Time of Turbulence

To better understand the pace and extent of change we are facing, consider the differences between the issues we dealt with in the late 1980s and those confronting us today. These differences are summarized in the table on the next page.

The table shows only a few of the recent sociopolitical changes that companies have had to deal with. However, the changes over the past decade have been even more dramatic. Consider some of the features of the 1980 and the current business environment for which our training and experience may not have prepared us.

Features of the Business Environment of the 1990s

Technology, customer expectations, global markets and global competition, blurred industry boundaries, constantly changing key success factors, and turbulent societal change have created a vastly different context in which companies are required to operate.

Technology

Technology is changing every facet of the way we do business. It affects organizational structures; the

1980s	Today
Societal Issues ■ United States and Soviet Union disarmament ■ Third-world debt ■ Japanese economic strength ■ Communism vs capitalism	**Societal Issues** ■ Collapse of communism and resurgence of multiparty democracies and nationalism ■ Economic reconstruction of Eastern Europe and the Soviet Union ■ Regional economic alliances—Europe, North America, the Pacifc Rim countries, and Africa ■ Market economies and the use of structural-adjustment programs to transform central-ized economies to market economies
Business Issues ■ The use of computer and telecom-munications technology to achieve a competitive advantage ■ Customers' demand for quality ■ Total-quality programs ■ Global competition from other companies in the same industry ■ Productivity improvements through mergers, acqisitions, and the resultant 'downsizing' ■ Affirmative-action programs to develop and promote minorities	**Business Issues** ■ Intergrated technologies that provide the ability to instantaneously transmit voice, data, graphics, and video worldwide, which will change the entire structure and nature of business ■ Customers' demand for value (i.e., a high-quality product at the lowest price) ■ Competition between spider-web alliances (i.e., companies in different industries and different countries, focusing on their core strengths) ■ Productivity improvements through outsourcing, joint ventures, breaking down of industry boundaries, business process reengineering, and the empowerment of employees ■ Multidisciplinary teams, multiskilling, and cross-cultural programs that enable people to work with people from other cultures and other disciplines

sequence and speed with which tasks are performed; relationships with customers, suppliers, and between departments; the expectations and demands of customers; and the skills required to perform certain jobs. The features of the new technology that have produced these changes appear below:

- Centralized Databases

- Global Networks

- Expert Systems

- Computerized Tracking Systems

- Automated Processes

- Process Reengineering

Centralized Databases

Centralized databases provide facilities for storage and retrieval of vast amounts of information from different departments and even different companies stored in one database.

Japan's largest food retailer, Seven-Eleven, consists of 3,900 franchises. Each franchise operates in only 100 square meters and carries a range of 3,500 products. The franchise owner knows exactly which products should be displayed on his or her shelves, at what time of the day, and which can be stored away. How does each franchise owner know which products to display?

Each Seven-Eleven store has a sales-point terminal. The check-out attendants use scanners to ring up the price of goods. Simultaneously, information such as the brand name, price, and manufacturer of the product, as well as the sex and age of the buyer, is recorded.

From a central database, the franchise owner is able to obtain graphs of the sales of certain products against hours in a day or days of a week. The owner can then ascertain which products to display on the shelves and when to do so. The franchise owner can also use the sales-point terminal to order goods electronically from the manufacturers, thus saving paper and time.

The parent company of Seven-Eleven is able to aggregate information from its 3,900 franchises regarding sales of individual products and it sells this information to the manufacturers.

Finally, corporate planners are able to obtain the following information from the database: who is shopping and when, how much they are spending, what they are buying, and how their tastes are changing.

The customer information stored in one central database can be shared by different companies. For example, travel agents link American Airline terminals in their offices to the airline's central database. This allows the travel agents the convenience of booking tickets from their own offices.

Avis's Wizard computer network is a database that can store information about 80,000 rental-car drivers. Each customer's car group, insurance preferences, and special requests are stored on a central database. Customers renting a car from Avis are able to obtain quick service. The company also uses the information for billing, marketing, administration, and better fleet management.

❝ *The customer information stored in one central database can be shared by different companies.* **❞**

Global Networks

Global networks allow organizations to transfer instructions, diagrams, and funds instantaneously between geographically separate organizations.

Toyota dealers in Japan have on-line terminals through which they can order cars directly from the Toyota factory. The dealers can specify individual customer requirements and book factory capacity from their own showrooms. The factory, in turn, is able to keep in touch with changing customer expectations. This not only allows Toyota to manufacture customized cars, but Toyota and its dealers can now carry less stock.

There are 500 hotels throughout the world that are linked in a single network controlled by Supranational Hotels. Customers staying at any one of these hotels are able to confirm reservations to any other hotel in the network within seven seconds.

Benetton produces more than 80 million garments a year. It owns seven production centers in France, Spain, the United States, and Brazil, and other joint-venture factories around the world. The company has agents in twenty-six countries and 7,000 shops. Its global network means that sales, distribution, and manufacturing sites worldwide can communicate with one another instantaneously. And shipping agencies in ten countries can transfer shipping documents electronically, which shortens the waiting at customs and speeds up delivery.

Expert Systems

Expert systems enable companies to capture and store specialized knowledge and expertise, so that it is available for simultaneous use by many people.

US West, an American Telecoms company, changed its organizational structure to one in which employees were made responsible for solving the problems of a particular group of customers, rather than fixing a specific technical fault. To help employees make the change from specialists to generalists, the company installed an expert system that advised the employees who to talk to in order to get various faults fixed.

The American Express Company's financial-planning subsidiary utilized the expertise of its best financial planners and developed a computer program called Insight. Using this program, it has improved the financial planning skills of its 6,500 planners.

Computerized Tracking Systems

Computerized tracking systems can automatically track the progress of a product or service through different departments or areas in a company.

Nissan, Japan's second largest car manufacturer, links its 3,000 factories and showrooms in a worldwide network. Through this network, any car part can be delivered to any part of the network within two hours.

In the United States a retail grocery chain has an agreement with a diaper supplier. The supplier contracts with diaper manufacturers to ensure that the grocery stores always have a sufficient stock of diapers. The supplier uses technology to retain its contract with the manufacturers. Whenever a shipment of diapers leaves the retailer's warehouse for a store, the supplier automatically notifies the manufacturers, thus enabling the manufacturers to produce and distribute exactly what is required.

Automated Processes

Cash withdrawals from banks used to be done through human tellers, but now automated teller machines are used. Currently, faxing, word processing, and photocopying are being done on different machines. Japan has developed the digital photocopier called Imagio, which can serve as a copier, laser printer, or fax machine. Linked to a computer, it automates office work so that a document typed on a computer can be sent as a fax, printed out, or copied with a single command to the computer.

66 Japan has developed the digital photocopier called Imagio, which can serve as a copier, laser printer, or fax machine. 99

Process Reengineering

Technology can be used to change the sequence of tasks in a process, often allowing for simultaneous work on a number of tasks.

In the past, factory machines could handle only one task at a time. Products were therefore produced in batches. Before each different operation or product, the machine had to be retooled. Retooling would take the operator between three and six hours. Each time this was done, the operator was required to test and adjust the settings, a process that resulted in costly scrap. Batch production on standard products was thus a prerequisite for low-cost products because custom-made products were too expensive and time-consuming to produce. Today, flexible manufacturing cells allow the operator to change, within seconds, the tools needed to perform any task. The system automatically selects the right tools from a rotating belt and inserts them into the spindles. This advance has introduced the concept of flexibility into production.

Traditionally, work was organized around the product. To enhance efficiency, work was sequenced according to departments. Once a department had completed its part of the job, the work would be sent to the next department. With the help of process engineering, work can now be organized around the customer. To shorten the time taken to complete a task, from the customer's point of view, tasks that used to move sequentially between manufacturing, sales, engineering, and support departments can now be done simultaneously.

Hallmark Cards Inc. provides a useful example of how process engineering has been applied to reduce the time needed to deliver new greeting cards and gifts to the market. Hallmark formed a number of teams consisting of representatives from its art, design, and sales departments as well as from suppliers. These teams listed all the tasks associated with producing and marketing each new range of cards. They then redesigned the process and sequence of these tasks so that a particular range could be brought to the market in less than half the usual time.

Future Technology

In the future we can expect further technological innovations such as hand-held personal computers through which we will be able to communicate with anyone in the world. Using these computers and global networks, we will be able to share drawings, photos, recordings, film clips, and videos as we talk with others. Face-to-face video communications will become the norm.

Customer Choice

As a result of these technological changes, customers have more choice. The flexibility that technology brings to organizations means that customers can now have "anything, anytime, any way." Customers now demand products and services that are designed/adapted to fit their individual needs.

66 Customers now demand products and services that... fit their individual needs. 99

A customer ordering a bicycle in Japan is able to choose from hundreds of different features and design his or her own personalized bike. The customer's requirements are sent from a terminal in the showroom directly to the bicycle factory where the computer designs the bike for manufacture. The customer receives the personalized bike a few days later.

This concept of customized products applies to every type of organization. Companies can no longer afford to offer only one standardized product. Even laundry detergent comes in a variety of fragrances.

Customers now expect high-quality customized products at a low price. Quality service is no longer appreciated, it is demanded.

Global Markets and Global Competition

Political and economic events begun in the 1990s, such as glastnost, the reunification of Germany, the reconstruction of Eastern Europe, and the economic unification of Europe, have resulted in the development of global markets. There was a time when you could tell what country you were in by the brands of goods being offered in the shops. Imported products were available at a higher price, but mainly French-manufactured products were sold in France and German-manufactured products in Germany. Today, products from all over the world are sold to markets worldwide.

Companies are also locating their factories outside their own countries and closer to their markets. Japanese car manufacturers are setting up factories in Britain. The cars produced by these factories are sold worldwide, even in Japan. Rolls Royce, a British engineering company, recently announced its intention to set up factories in the Far East.

> **&&** *Companies can no longer afford to offer only one standardized product.* **&&**

When companies do not want to relocate, they are forming alliances with companies in other countries. For example, German banks are merging with British financial institutions in order to offer a broader range of services to mutual markets. Rolls Royce is producing car components with partners in France, Spain, and Australia, and has recently announced a joint venture with BMW to build a factory in Germany. Nestlé has developed a number of joint ventures in its attempt to become a global company. It has an agreement with Coca Cola whereby Coca Cola globally distributes Nestlé coffee and tea. Nestlé, in turn, distributes cereals for General Mills, a company based in the United States.

Joichi Aoi, former chairman of Toshiba, sums up the movement toward global industries (Cross-Culture Communications, Ltd., 1991):

Tomorrow's technologies will require large investments in manpower and other resources that may be beyond the reach of any individual company regardless of nationality. Thus, co-operation in production, research and other activities will be the logical approach to developing and expanding new global markets.

Blurred Industry Boundaries

Not only are national barriers being blurred, but industry barriers are also dissolving. In the past, industry boundaries were clearly defined. The travel industry comprised airlines, travel agents, and hotels. The insurance industry was made up of insurance companies. Computer companies were the major part of the computer industry.

However, when a bank offers its customers a travel package linking airlines, hotels, and rental cars, is it still part of the banking business? When Sears, a department store, and IBM, a computer company, assemble a package of 4,000 electronic data services (ranging from home banking to restaurant reservations and grocery shopping) to offer to millions of telephone users, what industry are they servicing? When Hachette, a publisher of books, travel guides, and magazines such as *Elle* and *Paris Match,* joins up with Matra, a producer of missiles and electronic gear, what business will they be in? These two companies intend to combine Matra's skill in electronics with Hachette's knowledge of travel and entertainment to develop programmable portable phones containing information ranging from telephone travel guides to computer-generated maps.

Constantly Changing Key Success Factors

* ...competitors from different countries...are not necessarily following the established industry rules. *

When industries operated as separate entities, there were clear rules on how business was done that were understood by everyone in the industry. Insurance companies sold their policies through agents or brokers. Bank customers came to the bank to do their banking. Movie-goers went to the cinema to buy tickets. Customers paid in cash, by check, or by credit card for groceries bought at grocery stores. Estate agents represented property sellers and advertised houses and other property on their books or through the press. Certain key success factors represented the accumulated wisdom and experience of the industry. Industry people who understood and obeyed these rules were practically guaranteed success.

However, many of these key success factors no longer apply. New competitors from different countries or industries are not necessarily following the established industry rules. In Europe, insurance companies are selling policies using financial advisors, estate agents, and professionals such as lawyers. People now do their banking from wherever they are, using services such as Compuserve to link their portable computers to the bank's computer. Groceries can be ordered by computer and payment can be made by electronic transfer of funds from the buyer's bank account to that of the retailer.

Customers are no longer loyal to organizations that are well established in the industry. They do business with whatever organization meets their needs at any given point in time.

The rules for success in an industry are constantly changing. As competitors offer new products and services, and as customer needs change, so the key success factors alter. Successful companies now have to work very hard at tracking the changing key success factors and transforming their businesses in response to these. This philosophy of change is reflected by a sign hanging in the office of the chairman of Hitachi. It reads:

> Every day we make change and put words into action.

Turbulent Societal Change

The only thing certain about the world is that there will continue to be turbulent societal change. Consider the changes that have recently occurred: the reunification of Germany, the removal of apartheid in South Africa, the splintering of the Soviet Union, the Persian Gulf War, and the formation of the European Community to name a few. Each societal change greatly affects the business community. The Persian Gulf War affected the European tourism industry to such an extent that British Airways offered free flights to encourage tourism. The reforms in South Africa and the collapse of communism have resulted in new markets opening in Africa, Eastern Europe, and even the Soviet Union. Although we can be sure that societal changes will happen, the form these changes will take cannot be predicted.

Conclusion

In an environment characterized by innovative technological applications, changing customer demands, global markets and global competition, shifts in industry barriers, constantly changing key success factors, and turbulent societal change, the old rules for success no longer apply. Similarly, models of organizations that were developed for an era in which change was slow and predictable are no longer relevant. What is required is a new model that describes an organization in tune with its environment. A model of such an organization is the topic of the next chapter.

References

Morrow, L. (1991, March 18). Triumphant return. *Time, 137*(11), 18-23.

CrossCulture Communications, Ltd. The evolving mind of global management: 1. 1991. An inside view of Japan in a changing business environment. (1991, July 29). *Fortune, 124*(3), S1-S57.

2

A Model for a Versatile

Organization

The greatest chemist of all is nature itself, which never ceases to mix and combine, to break down or build up the elements of the universe in an infinite variety of chemical processes...

—*Robert H. March*

Introduction

The words we use to describe a business reflect our view of how that business operates within its environment, how it is structured, and what the rules are that govern its internal operations. Too often, we tend to use words to describe our organizations without considering the impact that our choice of words has on our thinking.

Hierarchy Diagrams

Imagine that you are playing Pictionary® with a group of friends. You are asked to draw a picture of an organization or a company. Would you draw a number of boxes arranged in a hierarchical structure like this?

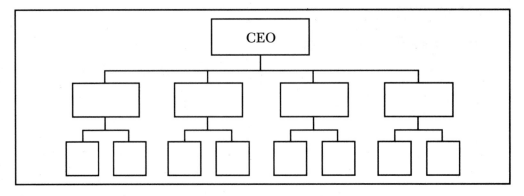

Or perhaps you work for an organization that is more customer-focused and, therefore, would draw something that symbolizes the fact that the front-line staff, who are closest to the customers, are more important than the chief executive officer. Does your drawing look something like this?

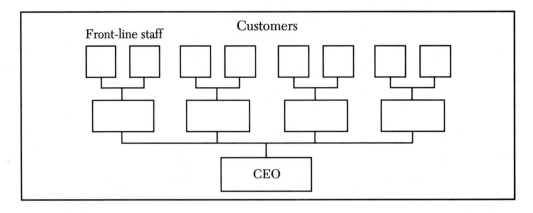

A diagram of the organizational hierarchy is a very powerful symbol. It conveys a message regarding the hidden rules and assumptions of the organization to the people working in the organization. Consider the two organizational diagrams. Each diagram represents a set of clearly defined boxes arranged in a definite sequence or hierarchy. What words come to mind when you see a picture like this? Clarity, structure, order, and fixed boundaries and compartments are some of the words usually associated with organizational diagrams. Are these the words you would like to have used to describe your organization?

The Versatile Organization

Think about the conferences you have attended and the books you have read that described successful organizations or "world-class organizations." What words or phrases were used to describe them? Words and phrases such as *flexible, versatile, dynamic, blurred boundaries, continuous learning organizations, customer focused, innovative, risk takers, quality service, systems,* and *integrating the customer* come to mind.

Are these the words and phrases that you would like people to use when describing your company? If so, it is time to create a new image in the minds of your managers and employees—one that allows them to act in a way that supports the development of a versatile organization.

The diagrams that are usually found in management theory books do not adequately describe what happens in versatile organizations. In order to find an appropriate image, I looked up words such as *change, system, flexibility, dynamic,* and *versatility* in dictionaries and encyclopedias. My search led me to the natural sciences where I finally encountered a diagram of an atom. Both the structure of an atom and the way that it operates within its environment closely simulate the way that a versatile organization interacts with its environment.

The concept of the atom can be used to explain the features of a versatile organization.

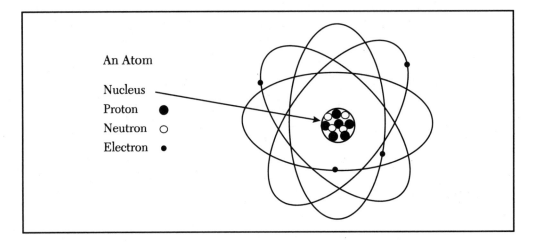

Some facts about atoms that are relevant to our image are given below:

- Atoms comprise three basic types of particles: protons, neutrons, and electrons.

- The protons and neutrons are clustered in the nucleus. The protons generate a positive electric charge. The neutrons have a neutral charge.

- Electrons, which have a negative electric charge, whirl around the nucleus at high speeds. They can revolve around the nucleus billions of times in a millionth of a second.

- The greater part of the atom consists of empty space. It is the speed of the electrons circling the nucleus that creates the solid shell-like appearance of the atom.

- Opposite electric forces attract. The positively charged nucleus exerts a force on the electrons to keep them in the atom; however, electrons have energy of their own.

- Electrons are arranged in layers or orbits around the nucleus. They fill the atom from the nucleus outward. If there are insufficient electrons, the outer layer remains incomplete.

- Atoms can combine with other atoms to form molecules. This process involves the sharing or transfer of electrons between different atoms. The nucleus remains the same. When different types of atoms combine to form a molecule, a chemical compound results. For example, hydrogen and oxygen elements combine to form a molecule of water; rust is formed by a combination of iron and oxygen.

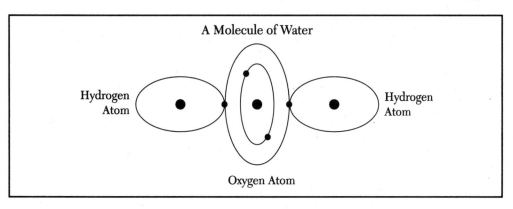

A Molecule of Water

Hydrogen Atom

Oxygen Atom

Hydrogen Atom

A Model of a Versatile Organization

When the analogy of the atom is transferred to the business world, a company operating within a turbulent environment could be represented in the following manner:

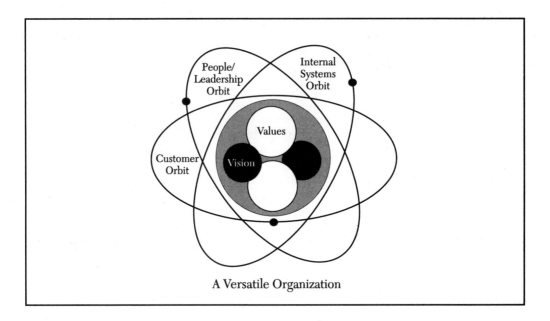

A Versatile Organization

Conclusion

Each component of the versatile organization will be explained in the next few chapters. Chapter 3 describes the nucleus of vision and values. In a versatile organization, the work that people do can be divided into three categories or orbits: (1) A customer orbit that involves all the functions that provide value to a customer; (2) an internal-systems orbit consisting of the systems and structures required for effective and efficient operation of the enterprise; and (3) a people/leadership orbit that creates the climate for innovation, flexibility, and commitment. These orbits are described in Chapters 4 to 6.

Reference

March, R.H. (1988). *World Book Encyclopedia* (Vol. 1, pp. 872-878). Chicago: World Book.

3

The Nucleus of the

Organization—

Vision and Values

We all grow great by dreams. All big men are dreamers. They see things in the soft haze of a spring day or in the red fire of a long winter's evening. Some of us let our dreams die, but others nourish and protect them, nurse them through bad days till they bring them to sunshine and light.

—Woodrow Wilson
United States President 1913-1921

Introduction

Continued changes in customer patterns, competitors, industry structures, and key success factors create pressure for people within organizations. When everything seems to be in a state of constant flux, people need some form of stability. Vision and values provide such an anchor for both leaders and employees.

The Need for Vision and Values

Whereas in the past, clear policies, procedures, and lines of authority guided decision-making, events that have never occurred before now require instant decisions. Jan Carlzon, of the Norwegian SAS airline, calls these events "moments of truth." These are the instances when a customer has contact with a baggage handler, a reservation officer, or a member of the cabin crew and needs a problem solved. Each customer's problem is unique and often cannot be anticipated or planned for in advance. Therefore, formal policies and procedures cannot be used to guide decision making. In order to solve the customer's problem, the employee needs to make a decision using his or her own initiative.

However, if everyone acted on their own initiative, the result would be a lack of direction, poor coordination, fear, and stress. In times of change, people need something that provides guidance and stability, without stifling the initiative and creativity required to handle the "moments of truth."

That something comprises vision and values. These are tools that define the what and the how of an organization. The vision defines what type of organization the company wishes to become and the values define how employees are expected to behave within the company. When faced with a situation that has never been encountered before, the employee must simply ask himself or herself, "How does the solution that I am now considering relate to the company's vision and values?" If it supports the company's vision and values, its "nucleus," the decision can be made with confidence.

66 ...formal policies and procedures cannot be used to guide decision making. 99

Benefits of Vision and Values

Clear vision and values have a number of benefits for versatile organizations. By providing a framework for making decisions, visions and values reduce the stress of dealing with unique problems and situations. Vision and values give top management the security of knowing that although it cannot control every moment of truth, its employees are acting much as top management would have acted in a similar situation. This is because the employees are making decisions in accordance with a common vision and set of values.

In order to achieve these benefits, vision and values need to meet certain criteria. These criteria will be described in the remainder of this chapter.

Visions

I have a dream that one day this nation will rise up and live out the true meaning of its creed:

"We hold these truths to be self-evident that all men are created equal."

I have a dream that one day on the red hills of Georgia the sons of former slaves and the sons of former slave owners will be able to sit down together at the table of brotherhood. I have a dream that my four little children will one day live in a nation where they will not be judged by the color of their skin but by the content of their character. I have a dream today and if America is to be a great nation this must become true, so let freedom ring from the prodigious hill tops of New Hampshire. Let freedom ring from the mighty mountains of

New York. Let freedom ring from the heightening Alleghenies of Pennsylvania. Let freedom ring from every hill and mole-hill of Mississippi. From every mountainside let freedom ring. When we let freedom ring, we will let it ring from every village and every hamlet. From every state and every city. We will be able to speed up that day when all of God's children, black men and white men, Jews and Gentiles, Protestants and Catholics, will be able to join hands and sing in the words of that old Negro spiritual, "Free at last, free at last, thank God Almighty we are free at last."

Martin Luther King, Jr.'s speech provides an example of a powerful vision. It provides a clear picture of the future as an event happening today. It is noble, inspiring, and motivating. On hearing the vision, people are inspired to contribute toward its attainment. Detailed decisions that need to be made are guided by simply asking, "How will this contribute toward the achievement of our vision?"

The chairman of Citizen, Michio Nakajima, describes his vision for his watchmaking company (CrossCulture Communications, Ltd., 1991):

Our goal is to grow far beyond our image as a watchmaker and use our ultra-precision mechatronics skills to diversify further into tomorrow's technologies. While we are number 1 in the world in watch production, we also want to be the number 1 producer of thinner, smaller, and highly specialized micro-electronic products for home and office use. We also want to become a truly global corporation that will be close to the hearts of people everywhere.

British Telecom's chairman describes the company's vision (British Telecom, 1991).

> British Telecom's mission is to provide world-class telecommunications and information products and services to develop and exploit our networks, at home and overseas, so that we can meet the requirements of our customers, sustain growth in the earnings of the group on behalf of our shareholders, and make a fitting contribution to the community in which we conduct our business....
>
> But we believe the greatest advantage will be seen over the longer term, as we continue to transform British Telecom into a company that responds instinctively to customer needs, and reaps the rewards in revenue and profit. It is by putting our customers first that we shall achieve success in an increasingly competitive marketplace, in the UK and worldwide.

66 *Many companies have been turned around by the application of an inspiring vision.* 99

Many companies have been turned around by the application of an inspiring vision. There is the famous story of Porsche. When Peter Schutz took over Porsche in 1980, the company was at an all-time low. The staff was demotivated and hostile. Morale was so low that the founder's son had moved out of the head office so as not to be associated with the company. For the first three months Schutz did nothing but wait. The workers began to wonder what was going on. Finally, the racing engineers met with Schutz to discuss their plans for Le Mans—a race that Porsche had won five times previously. They explained to him that because they had no chance of winning the race, they would go to Le Mans, not to race, but simply to market the new Porsche model. The new CEO's response was, "I don't care what you have to do, but Porsche is going to win at Le Mans."

The next two months were characterized by teamwork, excitement, motivation, and purpose. The story had a happy ending. Porsche not only won Le Mans, but also regained its pride. Schutz's vision had appealed to the employees' need for a sense of purpose and meaning in their jobs.

Rules for Creating a Vision

In order to be part of the nucleus around which the rest of the business orbits, a vision needs to provide answers to the following questions:

- In which markets will we compete?

- Who will be our future customers and what will they really need?

- Why will our future customers buy from us rather than from our competitors?

- What unique capabilities will we have that will give us the ability to meet our future customer needs?

- What will our organization have achieved that I can be proud of and committed to?

Communicating the Vision

Jung said that "A dream that is not understood remains a mere occurrence. Understood, it becomes a living experience."

Therefore the major question top management needs to answer is "How will I communicate this vision so that everyone in the organization understands it, is inspired by it, and is committed to it?"

In order to communicate their dreams, leaders use every occasion available to them to articulate their visions. Their visions are highlighted at induction programs, at retirement dinners, during branch visits, and in opening speeches at training courses. Every medium of communication is used to reinforce their ideas. These media range from videos, booklets, cards, cartoons, articles in the company magazines, and award ceremonies.

Values

Think of a company such as Marks & Spencer, a department store in Great Britain. How would you describe the company's products and services? Quality? Value for money? These values represent Marks & Spencer's approach to doing business and have become part of its corporate culture.

Jack Welsh, of General Electric, describes the values that he wished to develop at General Electric during the next decade. He hopes to build a company that (Stewart, 1991):

> ...is able to change at least as fast as the world is changing and [has] people whose real income is secure because they're winning, and whose psychic income is rising because every person is participating.
>
> And managers will be people who are comfortable facilitating, greasing, finding ways to make it all seamless, not controllers and directors.

A vision paints a picture of what the organization will be like in the future. Values give an indication of how people are likely to behave. Values answer the following questions:

- What is or is not important in the organization?

- What do we believe about our customers, employees, suppliers, and competitors and how will we treat them?

- What is our style of working?

- What behavior do we value?

- What are our ethics?

Every organization has values. These are the underlying beliefs that drive human behavior in the organization. Values affect the following:

- The manner in which people perceive or interpret events;

- What decisions are made and how they are made;

- What and who gets rewarded or punished; and

- Who is accepted and who is excluded.

Very often, the organization's values are not articulated or written down. People new to an organization often learn about these unwritten rules of behavior when they try to do something and are told, "That's not the way we do things around here," or "That's not the way we treat our customers." The organization's values are usually interpreted from the way in which top management

*** The organization's values are usually interpreted from the way in which top managment behaves... ***

behaves, its interests, and what behavior top management rewards.

Organizations that carefully consider, define, and articulate the values that they would like to see realized experience the following benefits:

- Values guide the decisions of employees at all levels in the organization;

- Values can be used to shape employee attitudes and behavior so that these support the organization's vision; and

- The organization's values, as seen in its culture, help the organization to attract and retain quality people.

An example of a clearly articulated value statement is Toyota's customer pledge, which is displayed by every Toyota dealer:

> We promise to:
> Treat you with honesty and courtesy.
> Conduct the repair right the first time or fix the repair free.
> Use only genuine Toyota parts.
> Show you the parts replaced.
> Have the vehicle ready on time, for work requested.
> Explain the work carried out.
> Not overcharge or conduct unnecessary repairs.
> Contact you after service to ensure satisfaction.

Levi's aspirations statement, on the next page, provides another example of clearly articulated values (Howard, 1990).

Aspirations Statement

Levi Strauss & Co

We all want a company that our people are proud of and committed to, where all employees have an opportunity to contribute, learn, grow, and advance based on merit, not politics or background. We want our people to feel respected, treated fairly, listened to, and involved. Above all, we want satisfaction from accomplishments and friendships, balanced personal and professional lives, and to have fun in our endeavors.

When we describe the kind of Levi Strauss & Co. we want in the future, what we are talking about is building on the foundation we have inherited: affirming the best of our company's traditions, closing gaps that may exist between principles and practices, and updating some of our values to reflect contemporary circumstances.

What type of leadership is necessary to make our Aspirations a reality?

New Behaviors: Leadership that exemplifies directness, openness to influence, commitment to the success of others, willingness to acknowledge our own contributions to problems, personal accountability, teamwork, and trust. Not only must we model these behaviors but we must coach others to adopt them.

Diversity: Leadership that values a diverse work force (age, sex, ethnic group, etc.) at all levels of the organization, diversity in experience, and diversity in perspectives. We have committed to taking full advantage of the rich backgrounds and abilities of all our people and to promoting a greater diversity in positions of influence. Differing points of view will be sought; diversity will be valued and honesty rewarded, not suppressed.

Recognition: Leadership that provides greater recognition—both financial and psychic—for individuals and teams that contribute to our success. Recognition must be given to all who contribute: those who create and innovate and also those who continually support the day-to-day business requirements.

Ethical Management Practices: Leadership that epitomizes the stated standards of ethical behavior. We must provide clarity about our expectations and must enforce these standards through the corporation.

Communications: Leadership that is clear about company, unit, and individual goals and performance. People must know what is expected of them and receive timely, honest feedback on their performance and career aspirations.

Empowerment: Leadership that increases the authority and responsibility of those closest to our products and customers. By actively pushing responsibility, trust, and recognition into the organization, we can harness and release the capabilities of all our people.

ℭℌℴ ℴℭℌ

Values of a Versatile Organization

What are the values that drive your organization? Whether or not your organization's values are articulated, it may be useful to test them against the values that characterize versatile organizations. These values appear in the list below:

- The future will be fundamentally different from today. It is not possible to rely on past experience. There is no "one best way" to do anything.

- The purpose of the company is to monitor and meet changing customer needs.

- Key success factors will change constantly.

- Hands-off management, empowering people, and delegating responsibility is essential for survival. It is not possible to control every interaction between a customer and an employee.

- People are expected continually to rethink how best to organize the system that designs, builds, or markets products and services.

- Change and movement are part of life and are to be cherished.

- Risk is part of any major change.

- Continuous learning is part of any environment in which adjustment is to be accepted.

- Innovation, speed, service, and quality are very important.

- Flexibility is needed in structures, goals, production, and so on.

- The satisfactory or adequate principle applies. Not everything can be perfect or proven before implementing a course of action.

- Innovative strategic planning, which involves thinking across boundaries and functions, is needed in an adjustment-oriented environment.

- The organization must be viewed as a system for any part of it to be understood. It is necessary to understand the interrelationships between components. No single aspect of the organization can be changed without impacting other aspects.

- Departmental barriers are fluid. Opportunities arise from sharing resources such as information, technologies, and skills across traditional departmental boundaries.

One of the key themes in a versatile organization is that of consistency among the environment, the vision, and the values. An example of consistency would be that of European companies who find themselves in a single European market. They need to have a vision of each of their companies operating outside their own countries and within this broader market. Their vision could include mergers or associations with similar companies in other countries. In order to support their vision, the companies would need to adopt new values such as learning other languages and studying other cultures so that they can better market their products in a multicultural and multilingual market.

There are general rules and concepts typifying versatile organizations worldwide, but the environment in which these organizations operate differs from country to country. Therefore, organizations will need to add the particular elements to their visions and values that will ensure consistency with changes occurring in their own environments.

Conclusion

Visions and values form the nucleus of versatile organizations. The vision defines the type of organization that the company wishes to become, and values define how people are expected to behave within the organization. Within the framework of its vision and values, each organization needs to produce goods and services that provide value for its customers. How to achieve this in a versatile organization forms the topic of the next chapter.

References

British Telecom. (1991). 1991 British Telecom's Annual Report.

CrossCulture Communciations, Ltd. The evolving mind of global management: 1. 1991. An inside view of Japan in a changing business environment. (1991, July 29). *Fortune, 124*(3), S1-S57.

Howard, R. (1990, September/October). Values make the company: An interview with Robert Haas. *Harvard Business Review, 68* (5), 133-144.

Stewart, T.A. (1991, August). GE keeps those ideas coming. *Fortune, 124*(4), pp. 19-25.

4

The Customer Orbit

Processes and people reconfigure perpetually to produce exactly what customers want and need.
                                        —*B. Joseph Pine, II*

Introduction

A popular definition of the purpose of business is the satisfaction of customer needs in a way that generates profit for the company. In order to do this, a company needs to produce goods and services that provide value for its customers. In traditional organizations a number of distinct departments and functions perform the work required to produce and market such products and services. Thus, research work is done by the research and development department, product manufacture is controlled by the production department, and marketing activities are performed by people in the marketing department.

In the versatile organization, the activities required to produce and deliver products and services are arranged in a customer orbit. The customer orbit has a number of features that differentiate it from the traditional organization. These features are listed below:

- Integration of functions;

- The changing role of specialists; and

- Development of generalist skills and the use of multidisciplinary teams.

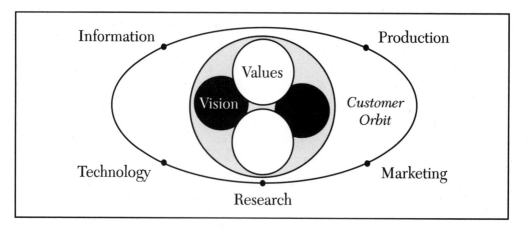

Integration of Functions

Within the versatile organization, the functions of marketing, information, research, technology, and production are welded together in a way that enables the company to design, manufacture, and deliver products and after-sales services that meet individual customer needs. Each function can be regarded as an electron in the customer orbit. However, as in the case of electrons whirling around a nucleus, it is difficult to tell precisely where one function ends and another begins. The teamwork between the functions in the customer orbit enhances the performance of the activities required to serve the interests of the company and those of the customer.

Identifying New Market Opportunities

Companies that perceive all activities related to providing value for their customers as one continuous customer orbit are able to do things that traditional organizations have difficulty in achieving. Versatile organizations find themselves continually monitoring changing customer needs and wants. They find it relatively easy to identify new market segments that arise from problem situations and respond by creating innovative products and services for these segments.

Identifying Opportunities from Problems

A few years ago, Yamaha, a Japanese piano manufacturer, faced a difficult period. Although it controlled 40 percent of the piano market, the market itself was contracting at a rate of 10 percent per annum. A traditional organization would have asked its marketing department to develop a new advertising or promotional campaign. Yamaha, however, decided to find out why people were no longer buying pianos. It combined skills from its marketing, technology, research, and production departments and formed a team. The team started by investigating how pianos were being used. It found that pianos in rehearsal halls, homes, and concert halls had fallen into disuse because people no longer had the time to learn to play the piano. Instead of creating pleasure, pianos were creating guilt.

Yamaha redefined the problem as "What opportunities could 40 million idle pianos create for the company?" By getting a multidisciplinary team to generate solutions to this newly defined problem, Yamaha came up with an innovative solution. Using sophisticated digital and optical technology, the team developed a product that could play people's pianos for them. The digital piano could record, on a floppy disk, each key stroke of a live performance, which could later be played in the privacy of the customer's home. This has created numerous new markets for the company. There are 40 million potential customers for digital pianos, diskettes of famous pianists could be sold to an even greater market, and as people listen to music on their pianos, many may want to learn to play the piano. Thus a market for tapes, video cassettes, and tutorials was created.

Another example has to do with record and tape companies. Traditionally, people who copied songs from records to produce their own tapes were viewed as "pirates" by the music industry. As such, they were considered threats to the profitability of the record and tape companies. Personics viewed the situation differently. It saw a market for using technology to create quality customer-designed tapes and compact disks. The company installed the Personics system in shopping centers. With this system, the customers are able to create their own

66 *Yamaha came up with an innovative solution.* **99**

CD's from a choice of over 5,000 song titles in the Personics library. Once the customers have chosen the song titles, their own tape or CD is produced within ten minutes with a personalized label and a list of the chosen titles.

Identifying Opportunities from Strengths

Often strengths in one area of a company can be used to solve problems in other departments. 3M is particularly good at exploiting its strengths and skills to develop innovative products. 3M's original business was adhesive tape. In producing this product, the company had developed skills in coatings, adhesives, and substrates, as well as different methods of combining these. By ignoring traditional departmental boundaries and thinking creatively about how to use these skills to develop new products, 3M was able to develop products such as Post-it™ notes, magnetic tape, and photographic film.

Integrating the Customer into the Company

When the Apple Macintosh was launched in 1984, it was not the best computer on the market. It had a black and white screen, a limited memory, and very little software to support it. But Apple had a major strength. It had a user group that privately provided the company with ideas on how to improve the Mac and publicly supported Apple. Ideas from the user group helped the company to produce a colorful, flexible computer that saved the product.

Providing Flexible Products and Services

In an article on why Toyota keeps getting better, Alex Taylor (Taylor, 1991) describes how Toyota can make fifty-nine models of passenger cars from twenty-two basic designs. Toyota's best factory needs only thirteen hours to assemble a car, as opposed to nineteen hours for Honda and twenty-two hours for Nissan. The Corolla, one of Toyota's high-volume cars, is ranked top of its class according to an independent survey. Toyota's use of the just-in-time approach allows it to manufacture only what is needed, when it is needed, and in the quantities required, whether this is a complete car or a single part.

Under this system, a car dealer will use an on-line computer similar to an airline reservation system to reserve factory time to produce a car. The customer is able to specify certain features and the factory then produces what is required within ten days. The just-in-time organization of the factory means that dealers do not have to keep a lot of stock, there is less wastage for the manufacturers, and Toyota is able to produce in accordance with demand. Just-in-time is more than a simple production process. It involved a total reorganization of every aspect of Toyota's business, including relationships with suppliers, dealers, and factories and a redefinition of roles and functions within its organization.

Integrating the Product and After-Sales Service

Xerox has used a combination of marketing, technology, and production to improve service on its

66 *Xerox has used a combination of marketing, technology, and production to improve service...* **99**

copiers. It uses technology to provide superior service to its customers in Europe. When Xerox was faced with growing customer complaints regarding the reliability of its copiers, the company interviewed customers to investigate the reasons for their complaints. When Xerox found that its machines were no less reliable than those of its competitors, Xerox decided that more research was necessary.

Xerox then set up videotapes in its customers' photocopying rooms to see how the copiers were being used. The videos produced dramatic footage of intelligent people becoming frustrated and confused when paper jammed the copiers or when copiers ran out of toner because these people could not interpret the complicated instructions on the flipcards attached to the copier. Xerox's later models, therefore, incorporated increased computer power. When something goes wrong, a picture of the problem appears on the display panel and clear instructions are provided for solving the problem. The results of these technological enhancements were dramatic. Where it had previously taken twenty-eight minutes to fix a paper jam, customers can now clear the jam in twenty seconds. The customers are, therefore, more tolerant of such breakdowns.

Xerox recently announced further service improvements. It can now preempt copier breakdowns that will require repair by a service engineer. Xerox developed a system of sensors that monitors the internal workings of each copier. These sensors (Remote Interactive Communications) are linked from the customer's photocopier to a central computer at Xerox. If the sensors find a fault, an engineer is notified. The engineer can arrange to visit the customer at a convenient time, armed with the correct parts, and fix the machine before it breaks down or inconveniences the customer.

The Changing Role of Specialists and the Use of Multidisciplinary Teams

In a versatile organization, the functional specialists in marketing, research, and production no longer operate independently of one another. In the customer orbit, the role of the functional specialist changes to one of providing other departments and team members with the tools, technology, techniques, models, or climate needed to help them meet changing customer needs more quickly, cheaply, or innovatively. The functional specialist works closely with people from other areas on joint projects, which may be permanent or temporary depending on the vision, values, and goals of the company. The following examples show how specialists perceive their roles in a versatile organization and how teams are used to meet changing customer needs.

Research

John Seely Brown, a director of Xerox's research center, believes that the role of the research department goes beyond simply innovating new products. "It must design the new technological and organizational architectures that make possible a continuously innovating company" (Brown, 1991).

To achieve this objective, the research center defined what research, technology, and innovation mean in a versatile organization. Whereas in the past, research had been defined as product research, the research center broadened its role to include researching ways to improve work methods through the use of technology and information technology.

In traditional organizations, innovation is usually considered the responsibility of the research specialist. However, Xerox realized that many of the best ideas came from employees who were solving work-related problems. The research center therefore redefined its role to that of "being a partner in innovation with employees of the company and its customers." With regard to its employees, it sees its role as that of challenging the thinking patterns and assumptions of people in order to encourage innovative thinking. Its partnership with customers involves the invention of methods and tools by the department to satisfy customer needs. This encourages the customers to identify their own needs, and the organization then co-produces, with each customer, the products that meet those needs.

Production/Manufacturing

The story of Toyota describes the changing role of manufacturing (Taylor, 1991).

> In companies in the United States, the production of a new car model typically begins with the product planning and marketing departments. The production head works under the instructions of these departments and very rarely has direct contact with customers or dealers. His or her role is limited to production.

At Toyota, all the functions needed to produce a new model fall under the supervision of a chief engineer. The chief engineer carries the responsibility for everything linked to the development of a car. This includes understanding the potential market by talking to buyers, developing marketing strategies, organizing suppliers, producing the cars, as well as staying in touch with social, political, and environmental trends that could affect the market or product.

The chief engineer encourages teamwork between different specialists. When a new model is developed, the production and manufacturing engineers work together to ensure that factory machinery is developed while the prototype is being tested. Thus the factory is tooled and ready for production by the time the prototype has been approved. Car engineers design parts in collaboration with body engineers, manufacturing engineers, and the stylist so that the parts can be made with fewer strokes of the stamping press. The end result includes less expensive dies, reduced operating costs, shorter shutdowns, and less maintenance.

This teamwork and shared responsibility to meet customer needs continues on the assembly line where the slogan is "Building the very best and giving the customer what he wants." Each worker is seen as the customer of the process that precedes him or her. The worker can expect and demand perfect quality from whoever works before him or her in the production process.

BMW has followed a similar approach. On discovering that engineers get 80 percent of their best ideas from casual discussions with one another, BMW decided to pool the resources of the product engineers (who design car bodies) and those of the factory engineers (who design the machines that make car bodies). BMW therefore took 6,000 engineers and support staff from ten different buildings and housed them in a $600 million research and engineering center.

Marketing

Regis McKenna, a marketing consultant from the United States, sees the following changes in the role of marketing (McKenna, 1991).

> Several decades ago, there were sales-driven companies. These organizations focused their energies on changing customers' minds to fit the product—practicing the "any color as long as it's black" school of marketing.
>
> As technology developed and competition increased, some companies shifted their approach and became customer driven. These companies expressed a new willingness to change their product to fit customer's requests—practicing the "tell us what color you want" school of marketing.
>
> ...successful companies are [now] becoming market driven, adapting their products to fit their customers' strategies. These companies will practice "let's figure out together whether and how color matters to your larger goal" marketing.

McKenna believes that the role of marketing has changed from getting an idea, conducting traditional market research, developing a product, testing the market, and launching the product, to a totally different concept of knowledge- and experience-based marketing.

According to McKenna, knowledge-based marketing involves gathering information about:

- The technology used in which the company competes;

- Its competitors;

- Its customers;

- New technologies that can change the rules of competition in the industry; and

- The company itself—its strengths, capabilities, and the way it does business.

This information is used to find ways in which to do the following:

- Integrate the customer into the design process to ensure that the company's product meets both the customers' needs and the company's strategies;

- Identify market segments that the company can dominate; and

- Develop relationships with suppliers, vendors, partners, and customers who will support and enhance the company.

Experience-based marketing involves spending company time with customers, suppliers, and competitors to find out how things work in the industry. This information is then compared with technology available within the company and strategies are considered to better meet customer needs, either alone or through cooperation with other companies in the same industry.

McKenna concludes that "marketing today is not a function; it is a way of doing business. Marketing is not a new ad campaign or this month's promotion. Marketing has to be all-pervasive, part of everyone's job description."

Technology and Information

66 Marketing today is not a function; it is a way of doing business. 99

The traditional data processing department's role was to process information or design systems to meet company requirements. This situation has changed and the department is now required to concentrate on establishing an adequate technological base. Adler and Shenhar provide two examples of this concept in an article entitled, "Adapting Your Technological Base: The Organizational Challenge" (Adler & Shenhar, 1990).

When IBM decided to compete in the personal computer market it already had the technological base it needed for success, the necessary computer and electronics skills, and a culture that valued technology, quality, service, and customer focus. However, IBM recognized that the personal-computer market required faster responses to customer needs than its existing businesses were providing. It therefore created a new strategic business unit that could operate in a manner best suited to the needs of its market. This allowed the unit to develop its personal computer exceptionally rapidly and win market share.

An example of an industry that did not have the appropriate technological base was that of the Swiss watchmakers. When faced with competition from digital watches in the early 1970s, the Swiss watchmakers were unable to compete. They knew very little about the technology of integrated circuits and digital displays. Their traditional structures prevented them from developing electronic devices. They did not have access to the appropriate project management or decision-making processes to deal with the much faster pace of technical, product, or market changes. As a result, the preeminence of the Swiss watchmaking companies was destroyed.

Conclusion

The customer orbit of a versatile organization consists of those functions (electrons) that enhance value as perceived by the customer. There is a nucleus of vision and values around which marketing, production, research, technology, and information orbit and are welded together to form a unit. It is difficult to delineate functions; however, specialists in each of the functions have a common purpose: to design, produce, and deliver both the products and the related services that meet the individual needs of their customers.

The element that provides a versatile organization with the flexibility to meet individual customer needs is the way in which its internal systems support change and flexibility. These systems are the topic of the next chapter.

References

Adler, P.S., & Shenhar, A. (1990). Adapting your technological base. *Sloan Management Review, 32*(1), 25-37.

Brown, S.J. (1991, January/February). Research that reinvents the corporation. *Harvard Business Review, 69*(1) 102-111.

McKenna, R. (1991, January/February). Marketing is everything. *Harvard Business Review, 69*(1), 65-79.

Taylor, A. (1991, November). Why Toyota keeps getting better and better and better. *Fortune, 122*(13), 32-49.

5

The Internal-Systems Orbit

Bit by bit, the forces of technology and economics are destroying the artificial constructs, such as rigidly hierarchical schemes for organizing work, that since the 19th century have limited the ability of people, organizations, and markets to behave in natural ways.
—*Stratford Sherman*

Introduction

Within every organization there are numerous intertwined systems that customers and outsiders rarely see. It is through these systems that the organization can operate effectively and efficiently. A company's internal systems can either promote behavior that is consistent with its visions and values or they can deter counterproductive action. They can also enhance or block the company's ability to provide optimal value for customers.

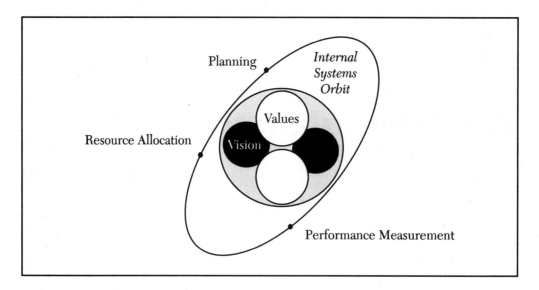

For these reasons, much of the traditional business education provided by universities and business schools revolves around the management of the internal operations of an organization. When anything goes wrong in an organization, the first area that consultants will examine is the internal systems—what is often called the "basics of managing a business."

The internal systems of a company have usually been developed to provide answers to the following questions:

- What do we want to achieve in the future?

- What needs to be done by whom, and by when if we are to achieve our goals?

- Which departments or employees get what resources?

- How do we measure and control the company's performance?

Internal Systems in Traditional Organizations

In traditional organizations, every function has its own systems and terminology that it uses to answer the four questions. For example, in reply to the question "What do we want to achieve in the future?," the finance people will discuss budgets and goals, the personnel people will discuss hiring employees and minority advancement issues, and the production people will discuss sales forecasts, production planning, and scheduling.

Have these specialists meet in a room and you will invariably find that, although they are all answering the same question, they are unable to communicate effectively. It is as though these specialists are speaking different languages—and indeed they are. Each specialist has learned a language and a set of rules that govern the answers to such a question. This is often the product of many years of study in a particular field. Each specialist answers a given question from the limited perspective of his or her field. These perspectives need to be integrated.

Each specialized function will develop sophisticated systems that answer all four questions in isolation of the other functions. Each of these systems is based on the theories and practices of a particular field of expertise. Thus, personnel systems are based on the theories of human relations, human resources, and psychology, and budgeting systems are based on the theories of finance. Specialists often will develop and refine their own systems without regard for the vision and values of their company.

Academics, consultants, and businessmen have invested a great deal of time and energy in developing, updating, and perfecting these systems. As a result, many of them have become highly sophisticated and deeply entrenched in organizations. In many organizations, the budgeting system is unanimously accepted as part of the way things are done in an organization. Although people will accept changes in structures, attitudes, and skills in the name of change, it is difficult to imagine telling a financial manager that the budgeting system no longer serves its purpose and should be abandoned. Imagine asking a personnel manager to eliminate the job-evaluation system. It would be difficult to convince almost any specialist in a traditional organization to reconsider his or her system.

And yet, many of the systems that are seen as the core of traditional organizations no longer function in a recognizable form in a versatile organization.

66 The versatile organization... is not driven by functions, but by visions and values. 99

The Internal-Systems Orbit in the Versatile Organization

The versatile organization differs from a traditional organization in that it is not driven by functions, but by visions and values. Like the customer orbit, the internal-systems orbit has a number of features that differentiate it from the traditional organization.

Integration of Systems

In a versatile organization, the systems for planning and implementing work, allocating resources, and measuring performance all form part of a single company-wide orbit that guides and manages the performance of individuals, departments, divisions, and the total company.

The Changing Role of Specialist Functions

The internal-systems orbit cuts across all levels and all functions. In traditional organizations, different systems are used to control financial, human, or informational resources. In a versatile organization, a common system and language is used for all of the systems and functions that relate to planning, implementing, allocating resources, or measuring performance. For this reason, the specialist no longer devises his or her own system in isolation. The specialist's information is simply fed into a larger company system that is driven by the company's vision and values.

Whether it be a company trying to position itself in a future competitive environment, a department trying to plan for the future, or an individual wanting to know about his or her future career path, they will all need to answer the following management questions:

Visions

- In what type of environment will I be working/competing in the future?

- To be successful in that environment what must I, my department, or my company be like? How can I meet my future customers' needs in a unique way?

Goals, Objectives, and Action Plans

- What long-term goals must I achieve to move me, my department, or my company toward my vision for future success?

- What must I achieve this year if I am to fulfill my long-term goals? What are my short-term objectives?

- What are the first steps I must take in order to achieve my short-term objectives?

Resource Requirements

- What resources will I need to achieve my short-term objectives and long-term goals?

Performance Indicators

- How will I know how well I am doing? What will I use to assess my own, my company's, or my department's progress?

> **❝** *In a versatile organization, a vision can be developed at every level.* **❞**

Developing a Vision

Chapter 3 describes how vision and values form the nucleus around which every aspect of the organization revolves. In a versatile organization, a vision can be developed at every level. For example, if the CEO has a clear vision of the total company, department managers could develop a vision of their departments being successful within the company's vision, and the individual employee could also develop a vision of himself or herself being successful within the company's and the department's visions.

But what if you are not a visionary? How do ordinary people at different levels go about developing their visions? The key involves answering the first two planning questions:

- In what type of environment will I be working/competing in the future?

- To be successful in that environment what must I, my department, or my company be like? How can I meet my future customers' needs in a unique way?

In order to answer these questions, you need to develop a number of visions. First, there must be a vision of the external environment in which the company will be operating in the future. Thereafter, a vision of the company competing successfully within its external environment must be developed. This vision needs to be clear so that any employee in any area of the business will be able to understand what is expected of him or her, so that he or she can contribute toward the realization of the vision.

A Vision of the Future Environment

Consider how the future environments of the company, the department, and the individual differ from one another.

From the diagram on the next page, one can see that at the company level, an analysis of the broad environment would be called for. This would include analyzing trends that would be likely to affect the company in the future. Trends in the following areas would require consideration:

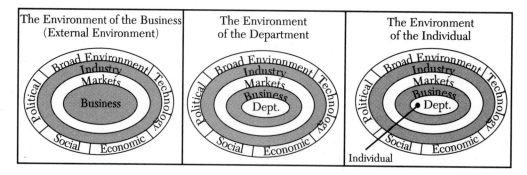

- The social, political, economic, and technological environments;

- The industry and its competitive environments; and

- The customer/market environment.

At a departmental level, an analysis of the company's vision would be added to all the above areas.

Similarly, the individual operates within the departmental environment, which in turn operates within the corporate environment.

Consider an example of how an analysis of the future environment can be used in the development of an innovative vision.

> When faced with the problem of a shrinking piano market, Yamaha could have used visioning as a different method of generating innovative solutions. An analysis of their societal, industry, competitive, and market environments would have revealed the following changes:
>
> - In the past, pianos had been popular as a source of entertainment, a way of creating music, and a means by which people could

play their own choice of music in the comfort of their own homes.

- Today, there are more sources of entertainment. People now spend less time at home listening to or playing the piano.

- Economically, people are better off than their parents ever were.

- People have less leisure time to spend learning to play musical instruments.

- Technology now provides people with more choices for listening to music. Portable videos, tapes, and compact discs allow a person to listen to music anywhere. The Personics system enables any person to design his or her own CDs. Digital computerized instruments allow people to create the sounds of a piano, drum, and percussion using only one instrument.

- Technological innovations in the computer and electronics field have created many exciting opportunities for combining technology with existing products in a way that could meet the customer's needs of individuality, flexibility, and convenience. The Personics system serves as an example.

This information about the environment can be used to develop a vision of the organization competing successfully within its environment.

Developing a Vision of the Future Organization

Once a clear picture of the organization's present and future environments is established, you will need to answer some further questions, bearing in mind the environment in which the company will be operating:

- What is the company's major strength: knowledge of a technology, such as digital electronics? a loyal customer base, such as that of the Apple user groups? ownership of an account customer base, such as that of Edgars? a superior relationship with suppliers, such as the one that Woolworths has developed?

❝ *People in...the organization need to...understand how they contribute to the vision.* **❞**

- How can I meet my future customers' needs in a unique way?

Yamaha's answer to these questions was to develop a strength by combining its knowledge of pianos with its knowledge of digital and optical technology, thereby creating a revolutionary new product—the digital piano. This product allowed customers to enjoy the benefits of playing the music of their choice on their own pianos without the inconvenience of having to learn to play the piano. This product also provided Yamaha with an entirely new industry.

Clarifying the Organization's Vision

In order to be able to use a vision to inspire people, the vision needs to be clarified further. People in different areas of the organization need to have sufficient information to be able to understand how they contribute to the vision. In clarifying the vision you need to answer this question: "If we were to achieve our vision, what would need to be in place?"

The following diagram shows the specific questions that will need to be answered before the vision can be communicated.

Expanding the Vision

Customer Orbit

- What products/services will the company produce or deliver?
- How will we design, manufacture, produce, and deliver our products and services to meet our customers' unique requirements?
- How will we structure ourselves to ensure that everyone associated with our customers works together in a way that best meets the needs of the customers?

Vision Core

- Who are our customers?
- What are their unique requirements?
- What are our strengths/capabilities?
- How can we combine our strengths to meet our customers' needs in a way that will entice them to buy from us rather than from our competitors?

Internal-Systems Orbit

- If our internal systems are to encourage the flexibility that we require to meet our customers' changing needs, what internal systems will we need to have? Which of our existing systems will no longer be required?

People/Leadership Orbit

- What types of people will be needed to provide the flexible, creative service we must provide?
- What leadership climate must there be to promote and support this flexibility?

A department within the organization could go through a similar process of developing a departmental vision. It could conclude by asking itself the following question: "Bearing in mind the environment in which the company will be operating and its vision for the future, how should our department operate if we are to contribute our skills to the company's vision?"

Similarly, the individual could develop a vision of what he or she should be like in the future if he or she is to contribute toward his or her department's or company's vision. The individual could specify the skills and knowledge he or she would use.

Goals

With a clear vision it is relatively easy to set clear long- and short-term goals for each orbit around the vision. The company, departments, and individuals can follow a logical process by asking the following questions:

- What must be achieved within three years to move me, my department, or my company toward my vision for future success?

- What must be achieved within one year if I am to achieve the three-year goals?

- What are the first steps I must take to achieve these one-year goals?

The diagram shows how this all fits together in a logical framework.

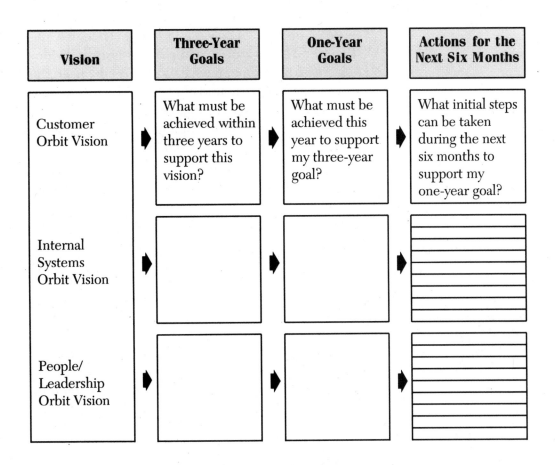

Vision	Three-Year Goals	One-Year Goals	Actions for the Next Six Months
Customer Orbit Vision	What must be achieved within three years to support this vision?	What must be achieved this year to support my three-year goal?	What initial steps can be taken during the next six months to support my one-year goal?
Internal Systems Orbit Vision			
People/ Leadership Orbit Vision			

In developing long- and short-term goals, the 80/20 principle applies. Choose only the few (20 percent) goals that will yield an 80 percent benefit.

Determining Resource Requirements

There is a saying that "a strategy is only a strategy when backed by resources." Yet, it so often happens that a group of people go away on a two-day conference in order to develop a vision or strategies. On their return, some of the more enthusiastic individuals try to implement what was agreed on at the conference only to find that there is not enough money in the budget or that people do not have the time, energy, or staff to implement the strategy.

The advantage of developing three- and one-year goals, as per the diagram, is that the following question can be answered at the planning stage: "What resources will I need to achieve my short-term objectives and long-term goals?"

If the resources needed to achieve a one-year goal are not available, it would be wise to admit that the three-year goal will not be achieved. As a result, the vision cannot be attained. The company should then be honest enough to remove the goal from its strategic plans rather than waste valuable time discussing strategies that will not be implemented. This honesty has the benefit of focusing people's efforts on strategies that are attainable and have been fully endorsed by the company.

> **66** *A strategy is only a strategy when backed by resources.* **99**

Performance Indicators

One of the questions that many organizations find difficult to answer concerns the measurement of performance:

- How will I know how well I am doing?

- What will I use to assess my own, my department's, or my company's progress?

In a versatile organization, where functions and systems are integrated into company-wide systems revolving around clearly defined visions and values, the performance indicators differ from the ones used in a traditional organization.

Subjective, Hard-to-Measure Variables

In traditional organizations, success was defined in financial terms. Financial indicators were used to measure the company's performance. These numerical indicators were objective and relatively easy to use. The same measures could be used to compare performance between different organizations.

However, these measures could not be used to track the progress of strategies relating to customer service and quality. New subjective measures, such as customer-satisfaction ratings and quality measures, were developed. In traditional organizations, subjective measures are perceived as being less important than the objective financial indicators.

In a versatile organization, the hard-to-measure, subjective performance indicators are perceived as being equally important to, and in some cases, more important than, financial performance indicators. Measures are related to the vision and goals of the company. In a versatile organization, the leader asks the following question:

> Given our vision and goals, what are the most important performance indicators?

As each company's vision is unique, the indicators used to assess performance would differ from firm to firm. In the Yamaha example the important measures for success would initially have been based on the achievement of the company's goals and objectives. Yamaha could include the following performance indicators:

- Skills developed in the fields of digital and optical technology;

- Knowledge of the market of piano owners; and

- Knowledge of competitor products in the field of creating and listening to music.

Once the product had been launched, further measures, such as sales, customer satisfaction, and market share, could have been added.

Similarly, innovative companies, such as Xerox or 3M, would require performance indicators for innovation, such as the number of new ideas generated from customers and staff. Volkswagen measures customer satisfaction and quality by obtaining customer feedback on the quality of its cars and service.

Focus on External Rather Than Internal Measures

Traditional organizations tend to focus on internal measures such as sales or profits. These internal measures are compared to the previous year's results or to current budgets. Variances against budgets are discussed and reasons for such variances are investigated.

Versatile organizations adopt a more external focus. They compare their sales, profits, and subjective measures to those of their most admired competitors or to the expectations of their customers. I recently had my car serviced. Two days after it had been returned, I received a phone call from a market research company retained by the garage. I was asked to compare the quality of the workmanship and service offered by this garage to services that I had previously been offered by any other garage. I was also asked to rate the extent to which the workmanship and service had met my own expectations. Needless to say, the service and quality that I had enjoyed was superior to any service I had received from other garages in the past.

This idea of devising performance indicators that relate directly to the company's vision, goals, and objectives can be applied at both a departmental and individual level by answering the following questions:

- How will I know if I am achieving my short- and long-term goals?

- What performance indicators could I use?

- Which customers could I ask for feedback?

Often, simply checking your progress against goals and objectives can provide sufficient feedback. However, on questions such as customer satisfaction, the departments/individuals could devise ways of getting feedback from their own customers.

Once a company, department, or individual has developed the following, implementation of the company's vision becomes easier:

- A clear vision of the future;

- Clear long- and short-term goals that support the vision;

- A knowledge of the resources required to achieve the goals; and

- Clear performance indicators against which the goals will be measured.

Implementation of Plans

Developing plans and goals is the easiest part of leadership. Putting those plans into action is more difficult. Alignment and role clarification are two useful techniques for implementation, and they need to be considered at the planning stage.

Alignment of Visions and Plans

The company's vision forms the framework within which departmental visions are created. In addition, each company goal should become the responsibility of a specific team. This team would develop its own vision of the contribution it would make toward achieving the company goal and also develop its own goals and objectives toward realizing its particular vision. For example, Toyota allocates the responsibility for developing a new model to a chief engineer and his or her team. Each individual engineer or production person in the team develops his or her own vision of the role he or she needs to play to contribute to the team's vision. Each engineer or production person then develops his or her own goals and objectives in relation to his or her role.

The Roles Needed to Achieve the Plans

The leader needs to ensure that the needed financial and human resources are available for achieving each of the goals that he or she has developed. The responsibility chart developed by Beckhard and Harris could be used as a tool to ensure that clear roles and responsibilities have been assigned for each goal.

For each major goal related to the vision, the names of people or departments who will play a role in the achievement of the goal should be recorded in the vertical columns of the table. The action steps relating to each goal could be listed in the horizontal rows. Finally, in a group session, the precise role to be played by each individual or department can be recorded in the boxes according to the following code:

R = Responsibility (not always authority)
A = Approval (right to veto)
S = Support (gives resources such as time, finances, skills)
I = Inform (should be consulted before action)

Actors / Goals								

The key to using the tool is to remember that not more than one R can be assigned to a task. Although many people can support or approve work done, only one person can be responsible for any goal or task.

This tool is especially useful in a versatile organization in which people working in different departments all contribute to the same goals. A great deal of frustration can be avoided by agreeing in advance on the precise roles to be played by each area or individual in attaining the goal.

Conclusion

Organizations often have clear visions and values. They try to structure themselves according to the rules of a customer orbit and make sure that their internal systems are in place. They have clear goals and the responsibilities for achieving those goals are clearly defined. And yet, months later, the goals have not been achieved. Many of the reasons for this failure can be traced back to people. Lack of support or sabotage by key people will impede achievement of any vision. The leader's role in creating a climate that is conducive to the achievement of the vision and goals forms the subject matter of the next chapter.

6

The People/Leadership Orbit

*The real difference between success and failure in a
corporation can very often be traced to the question of
how well the organization brings out the great energies
and talents of its people.*

—Thomas Watson, Jr.

Introduction

In Chapter 1, the characteristics of the environment
were described as changing customer demands,
global markets, intensive competition, collapsing
industry barriers, continually changing key success
factors, and turbulent sociopolitical change.

In Chapters 2 to 5 we found that organizations
that thrive within such an environment meet two
requirements:

1. They are constantly able to find innovative
   ways to meet individual customer requirements; and

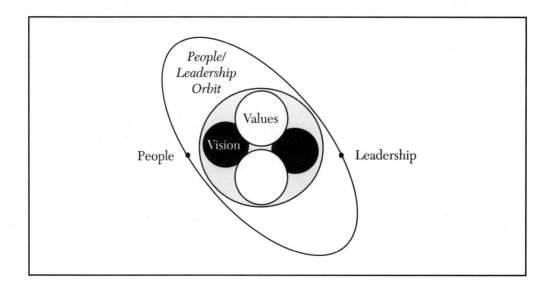

2. They are sufficiently flexible to change work patterns in order to meet individual customer requirements.

In a versatile organization, it is people, not products or technologies, that are able to make the instantaneous decisions required to meet unexpected shifts in customer needs.

What sort of person flourishes within a turbulent, unstructured environment? What type of person enjoys working with no other rule than the simple aligning of his or her actions to the visions and values of the company and satisfying the unique needs of its customers?

The literature calls them "empowered workers." But what is an empowered worker and what type of climate does he or she need in his or her job? What is the role of the leader in creating such a climate? This chapter addresses these questions.

The Empowered Worker

Let us do an exercise. Think back to a time when your abilities were tested and you passed the test. Perhaps you were writing an exam, being tested for a driver's license, playing a sports match, doing a presentation to the board of your company, speaking at Toastmasters, or writing a report that could make or break your credibility. Whatever you were doing, you needed to be brilliant on that day and you were.

On the day that you were to be tested you probably felt exceptionally nervous. But how did you feel later during the test, once your nervousness had subsided? People I have asked this question usually respond with words such as:

- Full of energy,

- Powerful,

- Confident,

- In charge,

- Alive,

- Smart, and

- Influential.

Employees in versatile organizations are put through similar tests every day. Every time these employees meet a customer or face one of Jan Carlzon's "moments of truth," they need to perform impeccably. They need to be charged with energy, power, and confidence. They must take charge of the situation and be alive, persuasive, and smart. This is the image of an empowered worker in a versatile organization.

If you don't believe that workers in your organization fit this description, there could be some good reasons. Remember the times you were tested and were successful. How did people treat you before you went "on stage?" Did you have someone who was supportive, caring, encouraging, and trusting? Did he or she believe in you?

What if, just before taking the test, you had been told any of the following statements:

- "You must follow the guidelines to the letter!"

- "Do it my way or else!"

- "We don't think you can do it."

- "We don't trust you to do it the way we would."

- "It must be 100 percent perfect or else you will fail."

- "If you make a mistake or if they don't like it, we'll blame you!"

How powerful would you have felt? Would you have felt that you were in control of the situation? To what extent would you have felt creative and flexible? If the people testing you had asked you to do something unexpected, could you instantaneously have found a way to adapt what you had prepared to meet their request?

Under these circumstances, the majority of people would be scared to make a mistake. They would fail to meet the expectations of those judging them by acting as most of our bureaucratic workers do today: inflexible, uncaring, unresponsive to customer needs, fearful of breaking the rules, and definitely not empowered.

If you could get to know some of these bureaucratic workers, you would probably find that some of them had been achievers in their personal, scholastic, or sporting lives. At some point in their lives, most people have felt empowered. Thus, every person has the potential to be an empowered employee. But do the organizations in which they work really want such employees?

The Traditional Manager

❝ *The behavior of empowered employees contradicts all the rules and values of the traditional organization.* **❞**

Traditional organizations find it difficult to accept empowered employees. The behavior of empowered employees contradicts all the rules and values of the traditional organization. Empowered employees question authority, they resent control, they do not follow procedures, and they do not seem to understand or obey "the way we do things" in an industry. They negatively affect what is most important to a traditional organization, order and efficiency. For this reason, traditional organizations tend to encourage conformity and discourage employees from being innovative and empowered.

In traditional organizations you will therefore hear managers say things like:

- ■ "We do things by the book."

- ■ "That's not the way we do things in this organization."

- ■ "We tried that once but it didn't work."

- ■ "We haven't budgeted for it."

- "If you're prepared to take the blame, go ahead."

- "You have to understand the politics before you can do anything around here."

- "I think we have someone else dealing with that."

- "You need to go through the correct channels."

And the employees respond appropriately, they do things by the book or are labeled as rebels.

The Versatile Leader

Leaders in any versatile organization realize that their success depends on having empowered employees who are committed to a common vision and values and whose common goals involve meeting the changing expectations of their customers.

Versatile leaders work at creating a climate that brings out the hidden power in every employee and at aligning this energy to the leader's vision and values.

Changing the Manager's Role

Jack Welsh of General Electric describes how he intends to change the role of his managers (Stewart, 1991) "from someone who plans, organizes, leads and controls to someone who facilitates, provides resources and encourages teams to think and act for themselves."

This new managerial role aims at fostering a climate to encourage development of empowered employees. Managers who have learned that the management function involves planning, organizing, leading, and controlling will naturally feel uncomfortable in the role of facilitator. The leader will need to encourage the manager and help him or her develop the skills required to perform his or her new role. To do this, General Electric has developed programs aimed at breaking down executive power and delegating more power to the staff by training middle managers in facilitation and process skills.

66 The leader uses his or her vision as a tool to inspire his or her employees. 99

Clear Vision

Leaders recognize that the first step to empowering employees is to give them a sense of meaning in what they do, a belief that what they do each day can really make a difference.

The leader uses his or her vision as a tool to inspire his or her employees. The vision would need to offer the employee an opportunity to contribute toward something great, something he or she can believe in. The leader would then spend a great deal of time communicating the vision to different work groups, showing how each employee can contribute to the vision, and what this contribution could mean both to the leader and the managers. It is amazing how much power ordinary people seem to acquire when they are working for a cause that they believe in. Whether it is a political fight for freedom or Porsche winning the Le Man's, an inspiring vision gives people a sense of meaning in their lives. This in turn releases an energy that enables ordinary people to do extraordinary things.

Values

Leaders recognize the importance of values in shaping behavior. They work hard to develop a culture that includes values that will empower people. Some of these values are listed below:

- The importance of helping customers to become aware of their own needs and helping them to satisfy such needs;

- Innovation;

- Change and movement;

- Risk;

- Learning;

- Service;

- Speed;

- Quality; and

- The ability to think across boundaries.

These are concrete values. Rewards and punishments are linked to behavior that supports these values.

Symbolic Action

One of the most difficult aspects of being a leader is living with the fact that the leader is always in the limelight. Whatever he or she says and does is interpreted as an indication of what the leader really thinks is important. Successful leaders recognize the power of symbols in reinforcing the messages contained in their visions and values.

Examples of symbolic behavior include those of Ray Kroc of McDonalds and Sam Walton of Wal-Mart (Hsieh, 1990). Ray Kroc showed his commitment to the value of cleanliness by picking up handfuls of trash from outside his restaurants before going in to talk to his managers. When Sam Walton took over as CEO, he initiated a cost-consciousness campaign. In support of this campaign, he did not spend money redecorating his new office. One of his employees commented that his office looked like "what you would expect to find at the regional depot of some truck line."

In order to convey the significance of how important flight punctuality was to him, Jan Carlzon used to observe the departure of flights from a terminal in his office. If a flight left late, he would phone to ask why. If a flight that had been plagued with problems left on time, he would phone to congratulate his staff.

> **" Successful leaders recognize the power of symbols...."**

Creating Legends

In his book, *Don't Ask Price*, Marcus Sieff describes an incident during which he acted according to the firm's values of caring for their employees (Sieff, 1987). One day he was told that a normally cheerful cleaning lady was looking depressed. A few days later she was still despondent and he was told the reason for her unhappiness. On their meager salaries, she and her husband had managed to put their only son through college. Their son had found a job in South America as an engineer and had fallen in love with a local girl whom he was to marry. The reason for the cleaning lady's depression was that she and her husband could not afford to go to the wedding. True to the company's values, Marks & Spencer gave her vacation time and paid the travel costs for her and her husband.

This story became a legend at Marks & Spencer. This simple act was a powerful way to transmit the message "We care for our people." Employees easily forget speeches and memoranda. The drama and the values behind a story such as this one are never forgotten.

Consistent Behavior

Consider the following saying: "To think is easy, to act is difficult. To act as one thinks is the most difficult of all."

Developing a vision and values is relatively easy. Acting out a company's vision and values is the difficult part of the job. The leader has to ensure that the messages contained in the vision and values and those demonstrated by his or her behavior and that of his or her managers are consistent. For example, a leader who preaches the importance of affirmative action and hires a new secretary of the majority race misses out on an opportunity to demonstrate his or her commitment. A leader who talks about the importance of meeting individual customer needs on one day and calls for a monthly report on customer-service costs the next day is conveying a mixed message to the organization. This will result in confusion or cynicism about the leader's integrity.

In assessing whether it is worthwhile to commit their time and energy to helping the leader achieve his or her vision and values, employees look for signs of the leader's own commitment to his or her vision and values. To test this commitment employees continually watch how the organization allocates its resources—its time, finances, and information.

If, as a leader, you preach the importance of affirmative action, customer service, or innovation, what resources do you allocate to these aspects of the business? To test the consistency of your words and actions, ask yourself the following questions:

- What proportion of your time as a leader is spent on communicating or monitoring your vision and values? How much time do you allocate to issues to which you purport to attach importance? How much of your time is invested in creating a climate that encourages innovation, customer service, or minority advancement?

- What proportion of your managers' and employees' time is spent on activities related to your vision and values? How much time is put aside for training, quality circles, and other interventions that will assist you in realizing your vision?

- What proportion of your budget is allocated to matters that you single out as being important? Do you have a budget for change management, innovation, customer service improvements, or minority advancement? Are you prepared to apply financial resources to projects that will help make your vision and values a way of life?

- What information do you receive? How many of the reports on your desk relate to matters that you have singled out as being important? There is an adage that people do what is *inspected* not what is *expected*. Are you constantly monitoring the activities that relate to the achievement of your vision and values?

Courage

❝ There are not many leaders who would order a change in the budgeting system to encourage... creativity. ❞

As a leader, do you have the courage of your convictions to act decisively against behavior that creates barriers for your vision and values? In a production plant, one obstruction in the production process can slow down the entire production line. Similarly, in moving your organization toward its vision and values, a single system, inappropriate structure, or conflicting behavior by key managers may undo all the effort you have invested in developing and communicating your vision and values.

In many organizations, the budget creates a major barrier to change, innovation, risk, quality, and customer focus. New ideas are often dismissed before they have had a chance to develop because someone says, "Sorry, but it's not in the budget." There are not many leaders who would order a change in the budgeting system to encourage rather than inhibit creativity.

How many leaders who advocate the importance of minority advancement would be prepared to publicly "punish" a manager who constantly blocks the development or advancement of minority managers?

Develop and Shape a Top-Management Team

One of the leader's major responsibilities is to surround himself or herself with people who will support him or her in reinforcing his or her vision and values. Like the leader, the top-management team is in the limelight. The team's behavior is constantly observed by its subordinates, who compare the team's actions to the words and actions of the leader. Does your top-management team comprise people who can help you create the climate you need to achieve your vision?

Conclusion

Although the traditional leader believes that *hands-on* management is a positive way to manage, the versatile leader recognizes that he or she can no longer control every encounter his or her employees have with customers. Yet every moment of truth will require instant decision-making and flexibility from employees. It is only with the support of empowered employees that a leader can be successful. The new leadership style has to be a *hands-off* leadership. This is a style built on trust, visions, values, and consistent leadership.

This style of leadership contradicts many of the values and rules inherent in traditional organizations. Most leaders have developed their skills and expertise working for traditional organizations. However, in many respects, the values and beliefs of a traditional organization contradict the behavior required of a versatile leader. The differences between the values of a traditional organization and those required in the versatile organization are described in the next chapter.

References

Hsieh, T. (1990). Leadership actions. *The McKinsley Quarterly, 4,* 42-58.

Sieff, M. (1987). *Don't ask price—the memoirs of the president of Marks and Spencer.* London: Fontana Collins.

Stewart, T.A. (1991, August 12). G.E. keeps those ideas coming. *Fortune, 124*(4), 19-25.

7

The Traditional Organization

*The man who builds a factory builds a temple. The man
who works there worships there.*
—Calvin Coolidge
United States President 1923-1928

Introduction

Our concept of an organization and the rules that
govern it affect our behavior, management, and
leadership. Our understanding of organizations is
derived from studies of management theory and
from our own experience in various organizations.
However, much of what we have learned, although
it has contributed to our success in the past, may now
prevent us from adopting the values and beliefs of
the versatile organization of the future. Until we
have consciously analyzed our personal values and
beliefs, the real transition to a versatile organization
is not possible. This chapter compares the values
and beliefs of a traditional organization to those of a
versatile organization.

What Prevents Us from Becoming Versatile Leaders?

A versatile organization sounds very exciting in theory. However, it is very difficult for leaders to adopt many of the concepts associated with a versatile organization. Some of the more advanced companies feel quite at home with concepts such as vision and values. However, the behavior patterns and internal systems required to complete the picture are not adopted. Leaders, managers, and employees find it difficult to embrace the type of thinking that is required to continually adjust their way of working to meet changing customer needs. Few companies can boast of having a truly empowered work force.

What prevents organizations from adopting the total package? What prevents them from becoming world-class organizations? The answer usually is not a lack of drive or hard work. What blocks the ability of leaders, managers, and workers to adopt the rules of the versatile organization is the organizational model that they carry inside their heads.

Think back to your first job. What was the organization like? How were you treated? How was it structured? What were the rules that you had to learn about how things were done? Do any of the rules in the box on the following page sound familiar?

These rules represent the wisdom of many well-known writers such as Max Weber, Frederick Taylor, Henry Fayol, Elton Mayor, and Abraham Maslow, who wrote about the rules for success for a particular type of organization that operated between 1900 and 1959.

Many of their ideas are still widely practiced today. Let us consider some of the features of the environment during that period and see how organizations adapted to suit their environment.

Rules in Traditional Organizations

- There is a hierarchical structure. Power and authority depend on position or expertise. Those in authority should be respected and obeyed.

- The organization is divided into functions. Finance, marketing, production, human resources, and data-processing specialists work in separate departments.

- Close supervision and hands-on management is the way to manage employees and prevent unnecessary mistakes.

- Efficiency is important. Employees need to follow predetermined procedures that represent the best way of doing things. These procedures are based on scientific research or past experience.

- We can always improve on the present. Employees should continually ask themselves "How can we function more efficiently and quickly or with fewer resources?"

- People are our most important asset. We therefore adopt a human relations approach of taking care of our employees.

- Everything is measured in relation to the bottom line. Ideas that will improve this year's bottom line will be adopted. Employees are rewarded for their contribution to the organization's quarterly or annual profits.

- Emotion has no place in business. Every problem has a logical solution. Anything that cannot be proven logically cannot be taken seriously.

- The future can be extrapolated from the past. For example, future sales can be forecast from current sales. From future sales forecasts, it is possible to estimate future costs, work force needs, and production capacity.

- One can simplify a complex task by breaking it down into component parts.

- Jobs can and need to be clearly defined. The activities of each job can be written up in a job description. If it's not in the job description I am not responsible for it.

Development of the Traditional Organization

The period 1900 to 1959 spanned two world wars, the Great Depression, the Cold War, and a period of economic growth and affluence. During this period companies such as the Ford Automobile Company, Daimler, Mercedes, Rolls Royce, Lufthansa, Uni-lever, Du Pont, BASF, and Hoechst were founded.

Inventions included the escalator, the rigid airship, the radio telegram, the wireless telephone, phototelegraphy, industrial silk, the first airplane flight by the Wright brothers, the washing machine, the theory of the atom, the tank, the Leica camera, the jet engine, Scotch™ tape, the helicopter, DDT, aerosol spray, the guided rocket, the Aqualung, the computer, the atomic bomb, the photocopier, transistors, television, commercial air travel, and satellites.

66 Business leaders and managers were able to focus their energy on increasing production. 99

Mass Production and Mass Marketing

In business, this was a period characterized by mass production and mass marketing. The development of technologies such as that of the production line and of management techniques such as scientific management allowed consumer goods to be mass produced at low cost. Products such as cars and washing machines, which had previously been considered luxuries for the rich, were now affordable for the middle class. The markets for consumer goods kept growing as a result of the following factors:

- Mass advertising persuaded people to buy the mass-produced products.

- Growth in industry created employment, which in turn created larger markets.

- Innovations such as credit and installment plans increased the demand for products.

Predictable Growth in Consumer Demand

Were it not for seasonal changes in demand, factory owners could predict with confidence that each year they would need to produce more than they had produced during the previous year.

The Business of Business Is Business

Political leaders such as Calvin Coolidge, a former president of the United States, recognized the benefits that increased production and employment brought to the United States, and he encouraged factory owners to direct all of their energies toward increasing production. The factory owner was not to be sidetracked by social or political issues. The business of business was business.

Internal Operational Focus and Predictable Competitors

Business leaders and managers were able to focus their energy on increasing production. This was done by improving the internal operations of their organizations. Although there was competition, these competitors were well known; they operated within the same industry and same country and used the same technologies. Above all, their competitors operated according to established industry rules. High consumer demand meant that there was room in the industry for both the company and the company's competitors.

Clearly Defined Key Success Factors

The key to ongoing success was to produce higher volumes at lower costs. This implied improving an organization's efficiency. Organizations were structured and managed with efficiency as the primary goal. Special- ization of work, functional structures, clear procedures, the production line, clear job descriptions, and unambiguous authority all contributed to increased efficiency. Increased efficiency meant increased production at lower costs for the mass market.

A Traditional Organization Versus a Versatile Organization

Now what happens if we superimpose some of the ideas and values associated with versatile organizations onto traditional organizations? What happens if we mix Table 1 and Table 2?

When faced with the turbulent environment of Table 2, many traditional organizations simply add some of the values and beliefs of the versatile organizations (Table 2) to their existing value systems (Table 1).

Table 1: The Traditional Organization

The Environment

- Mass markets.
- Mass production.
- Steady, predictable growth in customer demand.
- A few known competitors operating within the same country and the same industry.
- Clearly defined industry practices or key success factors.
- Stable technologies.
- Business that is immune from sociopolitical events.
- Expensive information technology.

Organizational Features

- Focus on internal efficiency.
- Specialization of tasks into functions.
- Large, hierarchical, and diversified.
- Simple production processes.
- Production line.
- Internal focus.

Beliefs About Business

- Business is a rational and logical science.
- Simplify complexity by breaking up jobs or tasks into components.
- The future can be predicted from the past.
- There is only one best way of doing things, which is based on scientific analysis and research.
- Specialization promotes efficiency.
- Mass production reduces costs. Customization is expensive.

Important Values

- Efficiency.
- Mistakes are unnecessary.
- Improve on the past and the present.
- Logical, deductive thinking.
- Short-term, bottom-line focus.
- The purpose of business is business (i.e., to enhance shareholder wealth).
- We do things for our people.

Table 2: The Versatile Organization

The Environment

- Turbulent societal change.
- Technology changes every facet of business and life.
- Increased customer choice.
- Demands for high-quality, customized products at a low price.
- Global markets and global competition.
- Blurred industry boundaries.
- Constantly changing key success factors.

Organizational Features

- Focus on meeting the individual customer's changing requirements.
- Blurred boundaries within and beyond the organization. Sharing of skills, information, and resources with customers and other companies.
- Continuous process of learning about customers and competitors.
- Flexibility and continuous redefinition of products/services, structures, and work methods to meet customer needs.
- Empowered work force inspired by the company's vision and values.

Beliefs About Business

- Business is like chemistry, the unique mixture and combination of skills and technologies to meet individual customer requirements.
- Complex problems need local solutions.
- The future will differ fundamentally from the past. It cannot be predicted. Key success factors will continually change.
- There is no right way of doing things. The way of doing things will constantly change.
- Companies must continually monitor customers' changing requirements with the help of technology. There is no time for traditional research.
- Customized, quality products can be produced at a low cost with the help of technology.
- Multidisciplinary teams are needed. Thinking across boundaries enhances creativity.

Important Values

- Innovation.
- Service.
- Speed.
- Quality.
- Continuous learning about customers and competitors.
- Flexibility.
- Thinking beyond traditional boundaries
- Movement and change.
- Hands-off management and empowered employees.
- Behavior that is consistent with the company's vision and values.

Conclusion

When change programs associated with versatile organizations are installed into organizations that retain the beliefs and values of the traditional organization, the result is increased complexity, confusion, and stress. The following chapter contains a description of an organization that is in the process of transition from a traditional organization to a versatile organization.

8

The Transitional

Organization

The toughest part is designing a new
organization while you operate the old one.
— *Jack Welch*

Introduction

Most organizations fall on a continuum somewhere between the traditional organization and the versatile organization. These transitional organizations retain many of the systems and structures associated with traditional organizations. Onto this base they have installed certain change programs associated with versatile organizations. The combination of these values and beliefs results in stress, confusion, and increased complexity.

The purpose of this chapter is to help you recognize the characteristics of a transitional organization in order to determine whether or not your company falls into this category.

A Case Study of a Transitional Organization

What follows is a case study of a typical transitional organization. The events and characters, though drawn from my experience in working with numerous transitional organizations, are all fictitious.

Each character in the case study will describe some of the stress factors that he or she experiences, and his or her views on what is important in the organization. From the narratives, you should be able to differentiate between those characters who act according to the rules of traditional organizations and those who believe in moving the company toward a versatile organization. Notice how events and change programs are interpreted differently, depending on the organization model the particular character believes in.

Inside the Transitional Organization

I decided to begin by interviewing the chief executive officer. It was difficult to set up an appointment with him; so when making the appointment, I asked his assistant to describe his job and a typical day in his life.

The Chief Executive Officer's Assistant

"A typical day is hectic. But he never has a typical day. Last week he was in Paris on Monday and in London on Tuesday. On Tuesday evening he flew to Amsterdam for a dinner where he gave a talk. On Wednesday he was back in London for a quick board meeting. Then his day was filled with meetings. At 10:30 a.m. he met with a manager to discuss operations and at 11:00 a.m. he met with the public relations manager to discuss the annual report. At 11:45 a.m. he had to see the editor of the company's news magazine and at noon he met the marketing manager to discuss the advertising campaign. He had a meeting with the training manager to discuss a new course at 12:30 p.m. and a management lunch at 1:00 p.m. At 2:00 p.m. he had a meeting with a group of company managers to discuss community issues and how our company should be involved. By 7:00 p.m. he was at a business dinner. In between all this we try to squeeze in telephone calls.

"Basically, his day consists of meeting after meeting. Everyone demands his time. So many people want to see him that he never has time to sit and concentrate or develop ideas. This creates pressure for me. There are so many questions that need to be answered and he is unable to address them because of his workload. He has to reply to queries and letters and get things done and he can't because there is not enough time. I have told him that we need to schedule in some time so that he can have restroom breaks! Because he is under pressure, he exerts pressure on everyone else.

"Of course, he loves his job. It is stimulating. No two days are ever alike. He gets involved in interesting projects both inside the company and with leaders of other organizations. Because of the people he meets, he is aware of what is going on in the country and so he is continually learning and growing.

"There are pressures from his family too. They keep phoning to ask him what they must do and how to do it. And then there's all he's had to give up. He can't see his children grow up. He feels extremely guilty about his family, especially when he has to miss a birthday or an important event. He feels terrible when he is away and they need him. Being away is not always glamorous. After a stressful day there is no one at the hotel who cares about his problems and talks to him about them. It gets quite lonely at times. That is, if he's lucky enough not to have a business dinner arranged for him that evening, in which case, his day ends only when the dinner is over.

"Of course, there is additional pressure when he cannot rely on his managers or when their subordinates come to see him with their problems. He has a constant stream of people who have to see him because they think he is the only one who can solve their problems or because they don't want to go to their own managers. And then there are individuals who need reassurance about the political environment. He gets invited to all those dinners so he should know! They all want to know how he sees the future."

The chief executive preferred to talk about the company and what he was trying to achieve.

The Chief Executive Officer

"You know the world we do business in today is very different from the one in which I earned my medals. Then it was easy. There were fewer competitors. The customers expected less. All you had to do to be successful was to choose between one of two strategies: to be the lowest cost producer or to provide quality products at a higher margin. Organizations today are faced with numerous pressures. There are the unions that insist on higher wages and greater company involvement in socioeconomic issues, the government that expects the private sector to fund more social projects, and customers who are demanding higher quality products at lower prices. The industry is more competitive. Profit margins are being squeezed. Some competitors are providing high quality at low prices. It's becoming increasingly difficult to compete simply on price. So how do we compete?

"My dream is that we should compete on the basis of service. I would like us to be recognized in five years' time as the company that provides the best service in our industry in this country. Now what do I mean by service? I mean that every time customers make contact with any part of the company, be it by telephone, by personal contact, or even through the computer, the customers should go away feeling satisfied. The customers should feel that they have found the best solution to whatever problems they may have had.

"How will this happen? First, this implies that the company has employees who believe that the customer is important. The employees are well selected on the basis of their values and are trained in how to treat a customer.

"We will empower these employees so that they can act in the customer's best interests. You know, employees on the front line can often understand customer needs better than we can.

"The employees will be innovative. This means that when one of our customers has an unusual problem, they will attempt to solve it without worrying about whether or not the solution conforms to formal procedure. Of course, this means that the employees will need different skills. The company wants to encourage employees from different departments to work together to solve customer problems in multidisciplinary teams.

"Now to make this all happen, the company has introduced some change programs and will introduce more later. There is the customer-care training program that teaches the employees the importance of the customer and how to deal with him or her. The 'customer is king' campaign rewards and recognizes employees in the company who provide superior customer service. Quality circles are aimed at developing participative management and innovation. There are multidisciplinary team meetings in which employees from different departments meet regularly to discuss multidisciplinary approaches to solving customer problems. Of course, we recognize that if our own employees aren't treated decently, they will not treat the customer well. For this reason we have developed a list of corporate values that describes how we treat our employees. And we look after the employees. The company has housing assistance programs, children's education policies, and the personnel department helps employees with any personal problems they may have and cannot cope with on their own.

"I have worked very hard at making these changes happen. I have spoken at conferences, time and time again, on the importance of what the company is doing and what is expected of everyone so that we can make this dream a reality. I have already traveled a million miles over the last six months!

"If the company can get this right, it will have a major competitive advantage. And that is why I'm giving up so much of my time to make it happen."

The Top-Management Team

We find the top-management team in its monthly meeting. Representatives include the heads of finance, production, marketing and sales, data processing, human resources, and the heads of the strategic business units, each of which controls a separate market segment.

While discussions around the agenda are taking place, let us look inside the heads of each of these individuals to glimpse at what they are thinking about.

Head of Finance

"It's okay that we are talking about all these warm fuzzy things, but we've got a business to run. Our costs are out of control. Once again, departments have exceeded their budgets and no one says a word. The company needs to keep its price increases below the rate of inflation and its dividends above it. The margins are being squeezed and the marketing and human resource people just don't understand this. If the company looks at its competitors, it would see that they are able to market the same products at much lower costs. Why? They appear to have fewer employees than we do and produce as much as we do. In this competitive age, the company has to find ways of making its employees more productive. I wonder how effective the middle managers are? There is a lot of dead wood in this organization. There is also a lot of duplication and wasted effort. The company needs to encourage its employees to find cheaper and more efficient ways of doing things."

Head of Production

"You know why the company's costs are out of control? It's because no one can make a decision. First, some managers say they want to keep costs low. I then tell them that the company needs to produce standard products. If they want all the frills and gimmicks to keep the company's customers happy it is going to cost more. I have to retool and retrain people and this takes time! And, of course, they never consult me when they start to design a new product. If they did, my department could show them how their new ideas impact the production process."

Head of Marketing

"Why do we keep talking about financial issues? I thought that our goal was to become a customer-focused company. How can the company be customer focused if it doesn't know anything about our customers? My department hasn't segmented the company's markets or determined the needs of each segment. So how can we offer superior service if we don't know what that means? I am about to launch an advertising campaign to promote the company's excellent service and I don't know whether the production department or administrative employees will be able to live up to our promises."

Head of Data Processing

"I can't seem to get through to them how much the company could save if it invested in better technology. The company is wasting so many resources. Information is collected ten times over. Each department has its own forms and information requirements. If only the company could centralize all of its information onto one database and analyze the systems so that information is captured only once, the company would save thousands of hours. But all the company looks at is the cost of the hardware and software."

Head of Human Resources

"Once again we're spending most of our time discussing financial issues. If the company really cared about customer focus we would spend time discussing ways of changing the culture of this company to a customer service culture. Also, at our last strategic planning meeting we all agreed that one of our most important strategies was the advancement of minorities. But we never get a chance to discuss it here."

Head of a Strategic Business Unit

"Listen to the other strategic business units' figures. They didn't do so well last month, did they? And yet, when it comes to budget time they get most of the resources. It's unfair. In fact, the company could save a lot of costs if each of us could run our own strategic business unit like a business and if we could get areas such as marketing and human resources to justify some of their expenditure.**"**

I then went to see the public relations manager to gauge her views on the company image.

The Public Relations Manager

The office is a mess. There are documents scattered everywhere. Ms. Peters, the public relations manager, welcomes me into her office with an embarrassed smile.

"Sorry about the mess, but I'm trying to finalize the annual report. Do you know how difficult it is to better last year's production? I need a new way of saying all the things that were said last year. It must look fresh, innovative, yet professional.

"Do you know what the hardest part of this particular job is? It's getting the copy in on time from all the people involved. The chairman's statement is a good example. This year he's writing it himself, but he is relying on information from someone in human resources and someone on the social responsibility committee. Of course, all this has to be integrated with the company's financial information and then all the different departments have some information to add to it.

"You know, what they don't realize is that I have to rely on about thirty people from different departments before I can do my job. I need information, art work, and photographs. And my requests are not the most important things in their lives. I have no power to force them to give me quality information on time. And I have to make sure that people outside the organization also do their part. Fortunately, I have an excellent relationship with the printers. They are going to have to produce miracles this year.**"**

In an attempt to discover what was important in the company, I asked her what image the company was trying to project.

"Well, top management wants to create an image of the company as a successful organization that has performed well in the past. So, of course, the financial statements will be shown. But it also wants to present a company that is well positioned to take advantage of any societal and industrial changes. So I need to demonstrate that our mission involves meeting the needs of all our stake holders (our shareholders, customers, employees, and business partners). I will emphasize some of the company's values, such as customer focus, innovation, and staff development and describe some of its strategies and the progress it has made in achieving these. These will include programs such as the company's customer-care program, its multidisciplinary team approach, its staff training and development, its suggestion-scheme competition, quality circles, the new computer, and the company's innovative products and services. Of course, I will also demonstrate the company's commitment to the community and its social responsibility programs. Then each department will be given some time to describe its products and services.

"As you can see, it is very difficult to put all this information together in a concise and attractive way. But that's my job, and I love it.**"**

The specialist's office was filled with pictures and cartoons that enhanced the atmosphere of fun and creativity.

I asked her what she thought of the company's strategies.

The Specialist

"I think that the company is on the right track with its idea of competing on the basis of customer service. Our department was involved in organizing the customer-care campaign. This is a campaign to encourage and recognize superior customer service. It consists of training courses to help employees understand what behavior is expected of them and why and will be followed up with a reward system to recognize employees who have provided good service for either internal or external customers. The company's in-house news magazine will be used to communicate, educate, and recognize employees along the theme of service. What I am finding exciting about this project is that it is the first time that the marketing and human resource departments have worked together. I am learning a lot from this interaction.

"Of course, it's difficult to sell the program to the middle managers. All they think about is production, productivity, sales, and budgets! But I do understand; they are under a lot of pressure. But then so are we. We have been told by top management that it wants the entire company to be trained in this program within the next three months. That is how important it is. **"**

I go down a flight of stairs, enter an open-plan office area and there, in the corner cubicle is the middle manager. There is someone in his office asking him how to do something. Another employee is waiting outside. As the first employee leaves, the manager asks the person waiting outside his cubicle to see him after our visit and then apologizes for having kept me waiting.

I ask him about his job.

The Middle Manager

"Well, the training courses teach you that a manager's job is to plan, lead, organize, and control. But it's far more involved than that. The workload in my department has increased substantially as a result of increased sales. I am not allowed to hire additional staff because the company has a freeze on new hiring—something about trying to keep costs under control. I wanted to hire temporary staff but I don't have the budget for it. Top management expects my people to attend numerous training courses on customer care and quality circles. I know it's important to top management, but I can barely manage with the people I've got as it is. Then, of course, management's minority advancement program is also important. I understand why it's important, but are you telling me that, with the shortage of trained staff that I have, I must now go and recruit a minority staff too? With whose budget? Where do I find the time to train the new employees? I have to help my existing staff with the workload. Do you know that I rarely leave the office before 7:00 at night? I use Saturdays to catch up on my administrative and managerial work because there is no time to do it during the week. My family is complaining that I spend more time at work than I do with them. But what can I do? Someone has to get the job done!

"What is important here? You tell me. The chief executive tells us that customer service is important. But when my department or other departments need the staff or the systems to provide it, we're told there is no budget for it. You know, if it was so important to keep costs down, why did the company spend so much money on a new computer? And how much did the company spend on those fancy consultants who are training my staff? Do you know what I could do with even 1 percent of that budget?

"Then every couple of months there is a new idea from top management. You know, I honestly believe that top management has nothing better to do with its time than dream up these crazy programs. First it was quality circles. My staff went to all the courses and put in time during its lunch hours to come up with an idea that would have saved the company a lot of money. We were all quite excited about it. My staff presented it to my boss and nothing has been done since. They are completely demotivated now.

"Then, of course, top management dreamed up these values that all of the employees are supposed to 'buy into.' There was a song and dance about how to treat people with dignity and respect. I liked these values until I saw one of the top managers shouting at her assistant. You just don't treat people like that. And then I thought that maybe the values applied only to us down here and not to top management. Oh yes, look at who just got promoted. You know how we're supposed to be a non-racist, equal opportunity company. Well, why do they promote people who are openly racist? How am I supposed to explain that to my staff and to the union?

"Top management's latest idea is multidisciplinary teams. Well, I went to one of these meetings and it was a waste of time. Each person spent time talking about how wonderful his or her department was. When I tried to open a discussion about the problems that my department has when working with other departments, I was told to stop being negative. Anyway, after the meeting, representatives from marketing and human resources said they were having a similar problem and that we might work together to try and solve it. But who has the time? When I did spend an hour with them, my boss told me that I should concentrate on doing my own job, not other people's. At the end of the day, we are measured by what our department produces against our budget. And so that is the 'bottom line' around here.

"Look, I would love to talk to you all day, but I have three staff members waiting outside with problems I need to solve. John is having trouble finding accommodation and I promised to help him. Peter needs some coaching on our new computer system and Brenda needs some information from me before she can carry on with her job.

"And then look at this in-box. The personnel department expects me to do performance appraisals on all my staff by next week. They also want to know how many of my staff have been to the customer-care program. The finance department wants my production and productivity figures and I must still find time to do my budget."

I left a very stressed man.

I managed to speak to a group of employees. I asked them what they thought the company wanted to focus on.

The Employees

"Profits. Profits and sales. So the managers can drive fancy cars. Actually, they are quite confused. They want sales to increase but that doesn't necessarily mean increased profits. The company needs to do more quality business. It needs to stop chasing short-term business and build up more credibility with its customers so that it can get repeat business. But to do that, we need support from the administrative and delivery staff. Our manager doesn't like this idea because he is measured every month on production and sales. He can't afford to lose a sale in the short term, even if it means extra business from a satisfied customer in the longer term."

"Costs are very important. If I want a new pen or correction fluid, I have to go and show my supervisor that the old one is finished. Yes, they certainly treat us like children here. And then they go and spend a lot of money on a new computer system!"

"We now have fewer people working in our department than before. We have to work harder and harder. All our boss cares about is productivity. And who benefits? The manager now drives a Mercedes. We are asked to work a lot of overtime. My wife isn't happy, but at least we get paid for it. But we really need more people in our department."

What did they think of the company's customer-care program?

"We think it is a great idea. The training course was very good and the trainer was excellent. It really opened our eyes. But is the company really committed to it? You know, we go to these courses and when we try to do the things we were taught, our managers won't help us. I had a customer who wanted something out of the ordinary. I could have arranged it for her, but it would have involved getting some other departments to help me. My boss said we couldn't afford the additional time, so I had to tell the customer no and she got it from one of our competitors instead."

"Of course, another thing is the values that top management spoke to us about. What's happened to that now? Why didn't top management keep them? We agreed with the ideas, but no one implements them. And the minorities advancement program is something else we don't believe top management is really committed to. It's just something it talks about to look good. For example, how many minority managers have we got in this company? How many minorities are being trained to become managers? Look who they promoted to senior manager, someone who is a known racist."

"And then, you remember we had that program called 'participative management.' There we were told to 'take responsibility' for our own jobs. But my boss wants to be involved in every decision. I have to tell him about everything I do. He wants to know about every problem, no matter how small it is. And if we do make decisions on our own, he doesn't support us."

"You have responsibility but you don't have authority. You are responsible for what happens but you are not allowed to change things."

Conclusion

The case study demonstrates characteristics found in a transitional organization:

- Innovative and visionary top management and specialists;

- Confused middle managers and employees;

- Different interpretations regarding what is important in the company from different departments and at different levels;

- Different interpretations regarding the meaning and significance of change programs occurring at different levels and between different functions;

- Lack of focus throughout the organization;

- Lack of synergies because of a lack of inter-departmental support; and

- Stress at all levels of the organization.

What can be done to alleviate the confusion and complete the transition to a versatile organization? This topic is addressed in the next chapter.

9

Managing the Transition

We are all on a spiral path. Now growth takes place in a straight line. There will be setbacks along the way...There will be shadows, but they will be balanced by patches of light and fountains of joy as we grow and progress. Awareness of the pattern is all you need to sustain you along the way.

—Kristin Zambucka

Introduction

Managing the transition from a traditional organization to a versatile organization requires careful planning. But more importantly, it requires a change in the hearts and minds of all the employees in the organization. It takes a courageous and versatile leader to transform the beliefs and values of any group of people. It takes a leader who understands how to manage change.

The Four Steps for Transition

Preparation for any major change, be it personal or organizational, involves four basic steps:

1. Picture yourself in the future.

2. Picture yourself today.

3. Develop plans to move from where you are today to where you want to be in the future.

4. Identify factors that will either block or support your plans. Develop plans for overcoming these barriers and building on your strengths.

1. Picture Your Business in the Future

This involves developing a vision of your company operating successfully within its future context. The concept of vision was described in Chapters 3 and 5. This section focuses on methods of developing such a vision.

Developing a vision involves the following:

1. Developing a vision of the future context within which your business will compete.

2. Developing a vision of your business operating within that future context.

Developing a Vision of the Future Context

Envisioning your business in the future involves developing a vision of the future social, political, economic, technological, business, and industrial conditions in which the company will operate. This is less difficult to do than it sounds. You can begin by identifying any trends that are likely to continue into the future.

Trends. A trend is simply something that is happening today and is likely to continue into the future. The following tables show the type of questions you could ask yourself in order to identify trends from which you can develop your vision.

Political Trends

- What are the global trends affecting countries worldwide (e.g., nationalism and market economies)?

- What are the political trends affecting your region (e.g., multiparty states or legislation on conservation)?

- What are the political trends affecting your country? How will global and regional trends affect the politics of your country?

Economic Trends

- What are the global economic trends (e.g., regional economic trading blocs, global economies, and global corporations)? What are your region's economic trends (e.g., tariff and trade agreements or structural adjustment programs)?

- What are your country's economic trends (e.g., employment, trade, foreign aid, and investment)?

- How will global and regional economic trends affect the economy of your country?

Social Trends

- What are the global social trends (e.g., life-styles, healthcare, housing, work habits, concern about the natural environment, and relationships)?

- What impact could technology and the global village have on people's lifestyles?

- What are your region's social trends (e.g., education, AIDS, health, housing)?

- What are your country's social trends? How will global and regional trends affect your country?

Technological Trends

- What are the global trends in technology (e.g., portable computers and global networks)?

Business Trends

- What are other companies in the same industry doing to become global competitors or versatile organizations?

  Consider the ideas contained in this book, such as leading by vision and values, changing the structure and culture of the organization, changing mind-sets and beliefs. Practice what General Electric did. Visit companies that you admire in other industries and investigate their "best practices."

Trends Within the Industry

- How is your industry structured? Is this changing?

- Who are your competitors? What products/services are they offering and to which target markets?

- Who are your target markets? How are their expectations/wants changing as a result of changes in global and regional trends?

- Who else from outside your industry is meeting your customers' expectations, needs, and wants?

- What joint ventures or alliances among companies from different industries are being formed?

Vision. From a study of these trends it is relatively easy to develop a vision. Try to visualize the future. Imagine it is five years from now. Picture the environment in which your company will be operating. You could use the following questions to guide your thinking:

Political, Social, Economic, and Technological

- What will the global, regional, and national situation be like in ten years time?

Business

- What will successful, versatile companies be like? What values and beliefs will drive the way these companies do business? What will it feel like to work in the versatile organization? How will leaders, managers, or employees behave in such an organization? How will it be structured?

Industry

- What industry will you be in? Who will be your competitors (both from inside and outside the industry)? What industry and inter-industry alliances will be in operation? How will technology or global alliances affect your industry?

Develop a Vision of Your Company Operating Within That Future Context

Once you have developed a vision of the future context within which your company will be operating, you need to develop a vision of your company operating successfully in such a future. The questions in the following table would need to be addressed in your vision.

Competitive Advantage

- In which markets will you or won't you compete?

- Who will your future customers be and what will they expect?

- Why will your future customers buy from your company rather than from your competitors?

- What unique capabilities will your company have that will give your company the ability to meet its future customer needs in a way that your competitors cannot match?

Values

- If your company is to be a versatile organization, what values/beliefs will you need to uphold?

- How will your organization treat your customers, employees, suppliers, and competitors?

- Which of the values and beliefs associated with versatile organizations will you have adopted? Which beliefs and values from the traditional organization will no longer be relevant?

Customer Orbit

- How will you organize the functions and activities in your company so that it provides direct value for the customer? What will the roles of each function be? How will employees work together? What relationships will the organization have with its customers, suppliers, and other companies?

Internal-Systems Orbit

- What systems will the company have for planning, implementing, allocating resources, and measuring performance?

The People/Leadership Orbit

- What roles will employees, teams, managers, and leaders play?

2. Picture Yourself Today

In order to be able to determine the gap between where you are now and where you want to be in the future, you need to compare where you are now to the vision that you have developed. The following table could be used for this analysis.

The Current Situation and Future Vision

	Vision	Current Situation
Competitive Advantage		
Values		
Customer Orbit		
Internal-Systems Orbit		
People/Leadership Orbit		

A problem faced by many leaders is that of obtaining accurate information about what is happening in their own companies. Managers often prevent negative information from reaching top management because they do not want to be perceived as not being able to cope or because they want to protect their leaders from the truth. The picture that top management has regarding what is happening in the business often differs from that of their employees. To obtain accurate information about your business, you should not rely entirely on what the heads of the respective departments say. Ask the employees who work with the customers or hire external consultants who have no interest in your company. The consultants can then interview employees at all levels and obtain an unbiased view.

3. From Today to the Future

❝ It is important to set goals within realistic time frames. ❞

This involves setting goals to bridge the gap between your current situation and your vision. When faced with changes that need to be made, companies often attempt to change too much too quickly. Although changes to products and systems can often be made within the space of one year, changes in values, beliefs, or culture will usually take between three and ten years to achieve. It is important to set goals within realistic time frames. The goals chart on the next page can also be used in the internal orbit and provides a useful tool for differentiating between short-, medium-, and long-term goals.

4. Factors That Block or Support

How often do you notice that excellent plans are simply not implemented? The leaders may do all the right things. They develop inspired visions and goals and they communicate these at every opportunity. And yet, when they try to measure their progress, they find that very few of the goals have actually been achieved. Let us consider some of the reasons for this.

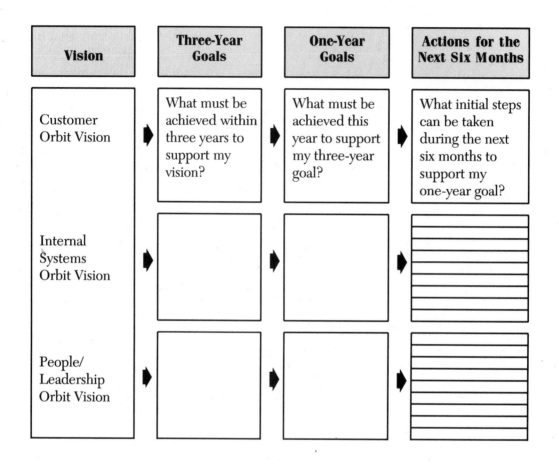

Vision	Three-Year Goals	One-Year Goals	Actions for the Next Six Months
Customer Orbit Vision	What must be achieved within three years to support my vision?	What must be achieved this year to support my three-year goal?	What initial steps can be taken during the next six months to support my one-year goal?
Internal Systems Orbit Vision			
People/ Leadership Orbit Vision			

A Belief That Change Can Be Bought

A major mistake transitional organizations make is believing that the change will be quick and easy. Bring in a consultant, buy a program, and the change will be effected. Few organizations caught in the transitional stage recognize that although money, changed management skills, and consultants are important in the change process, the leadership role in managing the change is more important. The greatest indicator of success is the amount of time, energy, courage, and perseverance displayed by the leader after the plans have been developed, because he or she is the only person who can do the following:

- Can constantly keep the vision in the minds of his or her employees;

- Has the power to remove obstacles to his or her goals and vision; and

- Controls the company's resources and can allocate them in a way that rewards actions consistent with, or punishes behavior that contradicts, the company's values and visions.

Organizational Systems

Why are the organization's visions or goals not achieved? Ask the employees or the middle managers and you will typically hear responses such as the following:

- "There was no budget."

- "Why should we? We don't get measured or rewarded for doing those things."

- "We don't know what is expected of us."

These comments reflect the fact that many of the internal systems that drive the organization were designed to support the values of a traditional organization. As such, many of the internal systems are in conflict with the values and beliefs required of a versatile organization. In some of the organizations I have worked with, barriers to the achievement of their visions and goals have typically been caused by the following systems:

- Budgeting,
- Performance appraisal,
- Goal setting,
- Communications,
- Rewards,
- Reporting,
- Job evaluation,
- Training,
- Career planning, and
- Organizational structures.

❝ *Lower-level employees will be quite open about the systems that are sabotaging your change efforts.* **❞**

To find out which systems in your company will support or sabotage your plans, ask employees at lower levels in your company the following question: "What do you think could prevent us from achieving our goals and visions?"

Lower-level employees will be quite open about the systems that are sabotaging your change efforts. Approach the specialists who control these systems with ideas on how to change them to support your visions and values, and one thing is certain: You will be faced with considerable resistance. You then have two choices: (1) You can either change your vision of what is required for future success or (2) you can change the deeply entrenched systems that are holding your business back. Sacrificing the vision is the easier option. Changing deeply ingrained systems is more difficult. In his book *The*

Prince, Machiavelli describes the courage that is required for changing deeply entrenched systems (Machiavelli, 1991).

> It must be considered that there is nothing more difficult to carry out, nor more doubtful of success, nor more dangerous to handle, than to initiate a new order of things. For the reformer has enemies in all those who would profit by the old order, and only lukewarm defenders in all those who would profit from the new order, this lukewarmness arising partly from fear of their adversaries who have made the laws in their favor, and partly from the incredulity of (people) who do not truly believe in anything new until they have actually experienced it.

Deeply Ingrained Values and Beliefs

The types of changes people experience can be divided into three categories:

- Things,

- Relationships, and

- Values and beliefs.

The easiest change to accomplish is that of things. Selling a house, buying new equipment, having a car stolen, or learning new skills are relatively easy to deal with.

Anything that involves a change of relationships is more difficult to accept. Thus, getting divorced or married, dealing with the loss of a loved one, starting a new job, or moving from one department to another causes a great deal of stress for all who are involved. People take longer to come to terms with any change that affects relationships. That is why the introduction of a new technological system with numerous benefits is often rejected or sabotaged by employees. Often those who introduce the new system fail to realize that the system may result in less contact between colleagues or that a new team of employees must establish new relationships.

The most difficult thing to change is the values or beliefs to which people subscribe. Have you ever tried to convince a wealthy person brought up during the Great Depression that he or she should spend money freely? How easy is it to persuade a religious person to give up his or her beliefs? Remember how long it took Margaret Thatcher, former prime minister of Great Britain, to develop a market economy and the strength that she had to muster to overcome the resistance to this concept?

This is the extent of the change that we are asking ordinary people in our companies to accept in making the transition from a traditional organization to a versatile organization. Paul Allaire, CEO of Xerox, described the extent of such a change (Dumaine, 1991):

> ...the hardest person to change is the line manager. After he's worked like a dog for five or ten years to get promoted, we have to say to him or her: All those reasons you wanted to be a manager? Wrong. You cannot do to your people what was done to you. You have to be a facilitator or a coach and by the way, we're still going to hold you accountable for the bottom line.

❝ *The most difficult thing to change is the values or beliefs to which people subscribe.* ❞

Conclusion

To achieve the benefits of a versatile organization, the organization has to undergo a fundamental transformation. This involves far more than tacking a few concepts such as vision and values onto the traditional model of the organization. It involves relinquishing the old beliefs, values, structures, and systems that have helped the organization to be successful in the past and embracing different values and beliefs that are applicable to the versatile organizations of the future. This involves courage, perseverance, time, and energy from the leader. Most of all, it demands commitment to making the company's vision and values a way of life. Such commitment is never easy. It involves pain, conflict, frustration, and patience to overcome the barriers preventing achievement of the company's vision and goals. And yet commitment also brings creativity, opportunity, and achievement.

We are only a few years away from the 21st century. Have you committed yourself to a dream for the year 2000?

References

Dumaine, B. (1991, June 17). The bureaucracy busters. *Fortune, 123*(13), 26-36.

Machiavelli, N. (1991). *The prince.* New York: Bantam Books.

INDEX

A

American Airlines, 5
American Express, 7
Apple Macintosh, 43
Atom, 20-21
Avis, 5

B

Benetton, 6
BMW, 11, 49
British Airways, 14
British Telecom, 29
Business environment, of the 1990s, 2
    blurred industry boundaries, 12
    changing key success factors, 13
    customer choice, 10
    global markets, 10-11
    societal change, 14
    technology, 4-10

C

E

G

H

I

- Editor:
  Pat Gonzalez

- Prodution Editor:
  Dawn Kilgore

- Interior Design and Page Composition:
  Judy Whalen

- Cover Design:
  Lee Ann Hubbard

This book was edited and formatted using 486 PC platforms with 8MB RAM and high resolution, dual-page monitors. The copy was produced using WordPerfect software; pages were composed with Corel Ventura Publisher software; and cover and art were produced with CorelDRAW software. The text is set in twelve on fourteen New Caledonia, and the heads are set in Stone Serif Bold and Bold Italic. Proof copies were printed on a 400-dpi laser printer and final camera-ready output on a 1200-dpi laser imagesetter by Pfeiffer & Company.